W9-CHP-424

15 Principles
of
Engaging
Leadership

Larry W. Dennis, Sr.

Rising Tide Publishing
Portland, Oregon

15 Principles of Engaging Leadership

Copyright 2014 by Larry W. Dennis
All Rights Reserved
Third Printing

Library of Congress Catalog Number: 2014920223
ISBN: 0-9844049-0-2
ISBN-13: 978-0-9844049-0-2

Cover design by Richard Ferguson, Ferguson Fine Arts

Rising Tide Publishing
10195 SW Alsea Ct
Tualatin, OR 97062

Engaging Leadership is dedicated to the empowering women in my life; my grandmother who loved me with unconditional love, my mother who thought I could never do anything wrong and my wife who has stood beside me, trusted me, and believed in me even when we couldn't pay the rent.

Also by Larry W. Dennis, Sr.:

Repeat Business:
6 Steps to Superior Customer Service

How to Turbocharge You:
6 Steps to Tap Your True Potential

Information in Formation:
How to Gain the 71% Advantage

Making Moments Matter:
89 Tools for Taking Charge of Your Time

15 Leadership Principles & Ronald Reagan:
Use Them to Change Your World

Motorcycle Meditations:
A Vision Quest to Alaska

Language of Leadership:
Communicating for Results

The Great Baseball Cap
(a children's book)

Table of Contents

Introduction: **Engaging Leadership**   1

Part One: **Preliminary Precepts**
Challenging Change   15
Synergistic Teamwork   29

Part Two: **15 Principles of Engaging Leadership**
Principle 1:   Lead from High Ideals   43
Principle 2:   Become Genuinely Interested   51
Principle 3:   Don't Criticize, Condemn, or Complain   61
Principle 4:   Provide Acknowledgement   73
Principle 5:   See Their Point of View   89
Principle 6:   Be an Active Listener   97
Principle 7:   Play Yourself Down   109
Principle 8:   Validate Their Ideas   121
Principle 9:   Dramatize Your Ideas   133
Principle 10:   Stimulate Competition   143
Principle 11:   When You Blow It, Show It   155
Principle 12:   Avoid Dogmatic Declarations   167
Principle 13:   Avoid Arguments   175
Principle 14:   Begin with Yes, Yes   191
Principle 15:   Appeal to Their Noble Motives   201

Part Three: **Continuous Improvement**
Practical Problem Solving   217
Leaders Are Learners   229

Notes   241

*Leading a team with low engagement
is like driving with the parking brake on.*

>>> **Introduction**

Engaging Leadership

While touring England several years ago, my wife and I visited Corfe Castle. The castle is a veritable fortress because of its unique positioning on the stone cliffs of England's south coast. Corfe Castle was the last stronghold on mainland England against Oliver Cromwell in the seventeenth century. Lady Bankes defended the castle against Cromwell's parliamentary forces for three long years. It was finally taken by treachery. A supposedly loyal insider opened a back door, permitting the opposing troops to penetrate the fortress and blow it up.

You may be granted authority by position, just as those who ruled ancient Europe. However, you will only experience true power when you earn the loyalty and engagement of those who support you. Engaging leaders have the ability to gain their associates' loyalty and enthusiastic engagement.

Regardless of your title, unless you are respected and have developed your ability to "bring out the best" in others, you will never secure the engaged cooperation and enthusiastic support necessary for results to exceed high expectations.

Produce Profits

Over 20 years ago, when I first met Greg, the president of a food service distributor, I remember saying, "Greg, you pay the same for gas, tires, and trucks as your competitors. The wage contract you have with your drivers are the same as your competitors'. In the vast majority of cases, the prices you pay for your products, from produce and dry goods to dairy and meats, is identical to the prices your competitors pay. The only thing that distinguishes you is your ability to somehow engage your team at higher levels than your competitors."

Greg's response was, "Absolutely. You're 100 percent right. By creating an engaged team, you win."

When Greg was appointed president of the branch, it had been losing over a million dollars a year. Greg stopped the red ink in his first full year, but was stuck at half the profit demanded by his owner. We explored what could be done to secure a higher degree of engagement and began the work that November. We continued working with his executive and expanded leadership teams over the next two years. Within a year, his branch's profits doubled and went on up from there. Nothing changed in their business model—no competitors went out of business, there were no dramatic market changes, no exclusive supplier contracts. What was different? *The aligned effort of an engaged, laser-focused team.*

My conversation with Greg occurred more than a decade before the terms "engagement" and "discretionary effort" became such an important part of management's vocabulary. At Turbo Leadership Systems, these words have been a part of our vocabulary for over 29 years. When we first introduced the *Leadership Development Lab* (LDL) in 1985, we needed a definition for the word "leadership." After turning to Webster and other authoritative sources and not being satisfied, we created our own definition: *bringing out the best so results exceed high expectations.* That's what creating an engaged team is all about.

The purpose of **15 Principles of Engaging Leadership** is to provide the insights, understanding, and tools needed to help you bring out the best so results exceed your highest expectations. Authority can be granted through position or title, power can be obtained through specialized knowledge, but leadership is earned. Leadership opportunities are available when you develop the ability to relate to, understand, and engage others.

Bullies

Don't wait for a title. When you take the initiative, you are the leader. Nancy told us,

> This past October, three young children from my neighborhood were shot at by a teenage bully with a pellet gun. This was just one in a series of attacks over the past couple of years by this youth and his brothers. In the past, my neighbors and I had lamented the fact that our children were being harassed, intimidated, and actually shot at. The police had been called to the home involved on several occasions; unfortunately, no permanent end to the behavior resulted.
>
> A neighbor and I felt frustrated by the situation and our sense of helplessness. We decided something more could be done rather than just notifying the police and talking about it. We thought it necessary to take action and get information out to our neighbors in order to allow our children to feel safe. My neighbor and I made up notices and distributed them door to door. We explained the situation (some people were unaware of any problems) and set up a meeting to discuss possibilities to make our neighborhood safe. We were ecstatic with the response: over 100 people showed up

for the first meeting. Once we were together, action came easily. People volunteered to organize and participate in neighborhood watch walks, cell phones were donated for use during the walks, the police became more responsive once we voiced our dissatisfaction over the past results of their actions, and the school and school board became more cooperative after we organized and presented a united front.

Three arrests occurred as a direct result of the neighborhood walks. Only one incident of intimidation occurred in the past four months, and a wonderful sense of togetherness in the neighborhood has been our reward.

The lesson I learned from this experience is that people are willing and able to accomplish great things. It just takes a little initiative and leadership by a few, and a group is able to accomplish more than individuals alone.

Whether you're appointed to a position of leadership or take a leadership role through your own initiative, your greatest challenge is securing the full engagement of those whose tasks must be seamlessly executed at high levels with minimum stress and frustration. Kevin Kruse defines employee engagement as "the emotional commitment the employee has to the organization and its goals." He says, "This emotional commitment means engaged employees actually care about their work and their company. They don't work just for a paycheck or the next promotion, but work on behalf of the organization's goals."[1]

Employee engagement means employees are passionate, excited, and committed to their work. David Macleod, an employee engagement expert in the UK, says engaging leadership "is about how we create the conditions in which employees offer more of their capability and potential."[2] Jim Harter, chief scientist at Gallup Research, says, "Engaged employees are more attentive and vigilant. They look out for the needs of their coworkers and the overall enterprise because they personally 'own' the result of their work and that of the organization."[3]

Measures of Engaging Leadership

Four measures of a successful engaging leader are associates who

- exert discretionary effort
- sacrifice for the leader's cause
- discipline peers
- align with the leader's vision

This is the definition of full engagement: *an alignment of maximum satisfaction for the individual with maximum contribution to the organization.*[4] The difference between engaged and disengaged employees is not a matter of work style or personality, and is not determined by the nature of their work. Engagement is based on a decision rooted in loyalty and commitment to you and your organization. Engaged employees are easy to spot—they are focused, results-oriented, productive problem-solvers. Engaged employees are excited and enthusiastic about their jobs, resist distractions, and routinely produce significantly more than their job requires. They encourage others to reach higher levels of performance and are proud of their organization. Engagement is a win-win relationship. Employees are getting what they want from their jobs, and the organization is getting what it needs from their employees.

Your business's primary purpose is not to make employees feel satisfied. Your business's purpose is to meet important human needs while maximizing the value of all resources at a profit. To do this, all employees must be meaningfully contributing to your organization's mission.

Fortunately, job satisfaction and engagement are closely related. Employees become engaged and satisfied when they accomplish results, know their contribution is recognized, and know they are fulfilling the mission of meeting important human needs.

An organization with high employee engagement outperforms those with low employee engagement. When you create engagement, employees are significantly more productive, customer-focused, and loyal. Elevating engagement levels drives improved organizational outcomes. According to Gallup research, organizations with a high level of engagement experience 22 percent greater productivity. Nearly $500 billion is lost each year in the United States due to disengagement.[5]

Employee engagement not only impacts job satisfaction and productivity levels, it increases loyalty to you, your department, and business. One of the effects of disengaged employees is the cost of high turnover.

There are many studies on the benefits of having an engaged workforce. They show direct lines between increased engagement and key business metrics. Benefits include

- higher productivity   *Beat the Bid!!*
- faster time-to-market
- more rapid innovation
- greater customer satisfaction
- lower turnover
- reduced absenteeism
- fewer accidents
- higher profitability

By contrast, leading a team with low engagement is like driving with the parking brake on. Things could be so much easier and get done so much faster if it were not for the drag caused by disengaged employees.

Your employees need to understand what is expected of them so they can apply their talents and get the results your organization needs. When they have the added understanding of how their job fits into the organization's overall purpose, they are better able to take the initiative, make timely decisions, and create customer-focused, innovative breakthrough improvements.

They also need resources and tools. Engaged employees understand which of the ten to-dos on their list take priority, and they have the tools, resources, and information they need to get their job done.

Feedback and development is another essential to high performance. To achieve higher levels of contribution, employees need to

- feel recognized and valued
- understand how they are doing on their assigned tasks
- be conscious of the strengths they can leverage and the weaknesses that are their liabilities
- find opportunities through formal learning or assignments to gain the knowledge and skills the organization needs now and in the future

Slammers

Jim, the owner and president of Hart, Inc., a Washington mechanical contracting firm, told us a wonderful, warm story about coaching his 10-year-old daughter's little league team, the Slammers:

The ball was being thrown all over the place. No one was catching the ball, and if they did catch it, they still failed to make their plays. The game was completely out of control. I thought to myself, "I am the coach. I probably ought to do something." To be frank, at this point I wasn't sure anyone could make a difference with these girls, least of all me.

I decided to apply my newly acquired Turbo coaching skills. I walked over to the first baseman and said, "I love your enthusiasm. If you hold your glove up high and steady to provide a clear target, and put your foot on the base before the shortstop throws the ball, you'll be more successful in catching the ball, tagging the runner, and getting an out. We'll win the game, have a winning team, and we can all go to Baskin-Robbins for ice cream after our win.

Amazing as it seemed to Jim, the next time the shortstop scooped up the ball and started to throw, the first baseman already had her glove held up high and steady. The shortstop threw the ball right to the glove. The first baseman kept her foot on the base and they got the runner out. Woohoo!

From that point, the game changed. Jim became a cheerleader with lots of "That's the way!" and "Wow!"—and a new tempo was set. To Jim's astonishment, the Slammers did win.

The lessons we can learn from Jim's experience are these:

1. Every member on the team needs a target—a clearly articulated, over-arching goal—"Win the game and go to Baskin-Robbins."

2. Performance standards need to be understood by each player: "Hold the glove high"; "Hold the glove steady"; "Keep your foot on the base."

3. Team members need to be given some helpful training: "Keep your foot on the base while holding the glove high—let me show you how." Training builds self-confidence, resulting in engagement. Training is seen as a fringe benefit; it builds morale and helps reduce turnover. Cross training helps build teamwork, esprit de corps, communication, and understanding.

4. Engaging leaders provide a pep talk of encouragement and support when the pressure is on. "You're playing with enthusiasm!" "You're having fun!" "Wow, keep it up!"

Jim's story is a superb example of how important it is to make our vision and expectations clear, to explain and document our standards of excellence. It's impossible for your team to read your mind and perform in the exact manner you expect unless you first make your expectations clear. You must clarify what excellence looks like. I have heard countless stories of employees who have been with the company for years, being moved from location to location, from position to position, and no one has ever clarified the standards for excellence. *Everyone has a right to know what excellence looks like.* If excellence is not understood, excellence will never be consistently performed.

To create an engaged, high performance team, there must be a clear understanding of

- the vision of victory
- the values for the voyage
- the company's goals
- the primary goal of their department
- the primary goal of their job
- the sub-goals of their job
- the standards for excellence
- the company's policies (A formal policy manual is necessary, but keep it thin!)

This is how you create engagement—by helping your team see how their work contributes to your organization's success. *15 Principles of Engaging Leadership* gives you the tools to do just that. The foundation of an engaged workforce is a workforce where each person can directly tie their work to the bigger picture.

Quota Buster

An organization's culture is its unique personality—the company's core values, ethics, and norms—the collection of habits of the individuals who make up the organization. Roger, shop foreman for a machinery manufacturer in southern Washington, shared an alarming example of the negative culture created when management allows disengaged employees to hold them hostage:

I was just out of trade school when I got a job with a Portland manufacturer as a production machinist. It was a good job with good pay. I enjoyed it and picked up the routine production system quickly. A few weeks into the job, the leadman came over to me and said, "There are only two things you need to know to be successful here—the first is that there are unwritten quotas for the parts you are running and you are never to exceed those quotas. The second thing you need to know is that management doesn't run the shop, the employees do."

I was dumbfounded. The unwritten "quotas" were so low, I could reach them in three to four hours. If I tried to go as slow as he wanted me to, it only made the job harder. Management was pushing me to get more parts out, and when I went over the unwritten quota, I experienced retaliation. My machines were being sabotaged, and the tires on my car were flattened. I was caught in the middle. Now instead of enjoying my job, I was miserable. I was always wondering what might come next. It became more and more clear to me every day that the inmates were running the insane asylum.

I couldn't continue in the direction it was going. Finally, I told the leadman that the only part of the job I liked was setting up machines and making parts. I told him if I could make quality parts faster than his "quota," I was going to do it. He got mad and said,

"You do what you need to do," and walked off. To my surprise, things changed that day. The harassment stopped.

To create engagement, be the kind of leader who inspires and creates a culture where *peers enforce high standards of excellence*—for safety, quality, and productivity.

When Jim, a long-time friend and client, read the above story, he sent us the following email:

> Shortly after I moved to Oregon to take my first job in radio at KTIL in Tillamook, I looked up John, an old high school classmate from Minneapolis. He told me he took a job running a simple drill press so he could coast through his workday and still be up for his night school classes. But he had quit.
>
> When I asked him why he had quit this easy, good-paying job that worked so well with his college schedule, he said that the forced loafing was too stressful. "It was hard not to do anything and still look busy when the foreman came around." I don't know about the other guys at the shop, but John told me he sensed they had no ambition, so a day of practiced loafing was good enough for them.

Wow, talk about disengagement!

How to Spot Engagement

ENGAGED	DISENGAGED
Attentive	Lazy
Responsible, Accountable	Can't be trusted
Energetic & passionate	Passive
Finishes work on time	Slow to get work finished
Rarely misses work	Absent or shows up late
Helps coworkers	Responds slowly to emails
Recognizes own strengths and weaknesses	Complains about work

Every employee, regardless of their role and responsibility, receives many messages each day that influence their mood, attitude, and engagement. These messages can include the company status report, goal achievements (or lack thereof), and feedback about individual performance from managers and peers.

Recognize that you can influence others positively as well as negatively. Start to change your organization today by connecting with your employees, making a commitment to rise above any negative noise, and proactively employing Turbo's 15 Principles of Engaging Leadership.

As a leader, you are the key driver of employee engagement. If you're not creating a fully engaged team, who will? You will successfully foster engagement as you make the 15 Principles of Engaging Leadership unconscious habits.

The benefit you will gain is the pride that comes from knowing you are creating an empowered workplace where good people find fulfillment.

>>>Part One

Preliminary Precepts

Challenging Change

Gene Faber, the great French naturalist, discovered the perfect example of habitual, unconscious behavior while studying processionary caterpillars. These unique creatures spend their lives in the forest feeding on pine needles. They move among the trees in a long chain with their eyes half closed and their heads butted closely against the caterpillar just ahead of them in a sort of bumper-to-bumper fashion.

Faber wondered, "What would happen if I connected the leader to the last caterpillar in the chain?" Without much trouble, he succeeded in getting a circle going around the rim of a flower pot. Around and around the caterpillars went, for seven days and seven nights. Nothing could break the chain, except exhaustion and weakness from lack of food. And yet food was there in the middle of the pot less than a caterpillar-length away, a feast for everybody if only one of the caterpillars would break the chain, but none of them did. Managers who don't change and who don't encourage change are like the processionary caterpillars. They don't get anywhere important, and they don't lead their team to results that exceed high expectations. In the world of change that confronts us, they are as outdated as the rotary telephone.

If your current practices aren't having the results you want, don't keep hoping that someday they will. Dare to try something new. Change is necessary for wellbeing and success—your own, your team's, and your company's.

Three-Point Trophy

Mark, supervisor for a Clark County commercial plumbing contractor, told us,

After fifteen years of elk hunting, I finally got my first elk—not the biggest elk in the world—only a 3 x 3. Even though the rack is small, it has important meaning to me.

My dad taught me how to hunt, and for the first several years, I did exactly what he taught me to do—walked a certain way, followed a specific route, and did things the same every season with the same results—nothing. I didn't even see an elk, nothing!

Then I realized that even though my dad has done some really amazing things in his life and has taught me more than he will ever realize, hunting elk is just not one of his strengths. He has only gotten one bull elk in his entire life and it was a spike. He was stuck in a rut that wasn't working and I was right there with him.

I decided to start mixing things up. I changed the way I walked and how I moved through the woods. I started learning the animal's habits. These changes—some successful, some not—led me to more sightings and more interactions, which led to more learning; more and more sightings each year until I actually might have gotten my first bull, but the timing just wasn't quite right. On the last day of elk season in 2005, my dad and I had just finished our lunch and were looking out the truck window at the downpour outside. My dad said he was staying in the truck. I said, "Bag that. I'm not going to get anything sitting in the truck." Minutes into the woods, there he was. Boom! My first elk!

This experience taught me some very valuable life lessons: I learned that adaptation and persistence pay off. It's not enough to just keep trying. I must learn, change, and adapt to win. My goals may take a little longer to achieve than I first thought, but with persistence and a willingness to adapt, learn, and change, I can definitely achieve my goals.

Me First

Don, plant superintendent for an apple chip processing company in Yakima, WA, told us,

I needed our processing lead to expand his role as a supervisor. As I reviewed his approach to problems, changes, and initiatives, it occurred to me that I could help him step up to the expanding responsibility if I could change my approach. I could see that if I changed my communication and leadership style from a direct command approach to a friendlier, more helpful, consultative approach, it would help him take greater ownership of the success of our overall operation.

Now when I hand off an assignment or tell him about a change in his area, I explain the benefits along with the ramifications of his actions. I am giving him a lot more background on why we need to accomplish many of the changed and expanded tasks that have recently been given to his department.

Over the past four weeks, I have been applying several of the 15 Principles of Engaging Leadership. Working to "See Their Point of View" (#5) required that I "Be an Active Listener" (#6). I also used "Validate Their Ideas" (#8), and when our processing lead used his ideas to move things forward, I lavishly used "Provide Acknowledgement (#4).

I can see the needed performance changes beginning to evolve within the crew. There's a greater emphasis on attention to detail. He and his crew have turned the corner.

I believe he has a much better understanding of what changes he must make in his operation, and more importantly, why these changes matter.

The lesson I learned from this experience is to evaluate *my* performance—how I approach my team—first. Before I ask anyone else to change, I need to be sure *I* am willing to change.

Leaders Are Responsible for the Future

Joel Barker, author of *Future Edge*, says the role of leaders in change is inestimable. "If you think about it," Barker says, "the responsibility of leaders is almost nowhere in the present. It's about finding the future for their corporation. The key word is anticipation. That's what separates the leader and the follower—the leader has the ability to anticipate the future."[6]

In "Marketing Myopia," one of the most talked about articles ever published in *Harvard Business Review*, Theodore Levitt said, "Most managers manage for yesterday's conditions, because yesterday is where they got their experiences and had their successes. But leadership is about tomorrow, not yesterday."[7]

Engaging leaders see innovation and invention as their primary job. You must be more than the caretaker of a legacy or a manager of a practice. Your job is not incremental improvements. Incremental improvements are the job of the front line. Yes, you encourage incremental improvements; you craft a culture that ensures incremental frontline improvements are a way of life, but you don't see it as your job to create these continual improvements in sourcing, finance, human resources, supply chain logistics, information systems, engineering, manufacturing, sales, and marketing.

Your job is not finding ways to create *reasonable* profits, profits that are equal to or a little better than industry norms.

Instead, as a leader, you see it as your job to create dramatic breakthroughs in product innovation, distribution, and finance, to create a team that is fully engaged in forward motion. You see it as your job to ensure that *no* energy is lost in internal turf battles or competition for attention. Instead you create an organization where open communication and trust abounds. The focus is forward; the questions on everyone's mind are "How can we serve our customers at higher levels?" "How can we be 'Best in Class,' the industry benchmark?" "How can we secure dominant market share in our chosen niche?" and "How can we secure new markets to increase our sales?"

You move beyond the practices, methods, and disciplines of the managers who preceded you. The status quo is not an option. You will be purchased, forced out of business, or you will grow and purchase or replace your competitors. Start today: get out of the box by questioning every assumption.

Three Approaches to Change

There are three approaches to change: you can initiate, cooperate with, or resist change. People who initiate change, who are pioneers of change, break through old traditions, old routines, old methods, and approaches. Pioneers of change are out front. They include Louis Pasteur, Marie Curie, Thomas Edison, Henry Ford, Alexander Graham Bell, Ada Lovelace, Sally Ride, Indira Ghandi, Mark Zuckerberg, Steve Jobs, and Elon Musk. The wealth of the world is multiplied by these pioneers of change.

The second approach to change is to cooperate. We go along with change as long as it isn't too new, too difficult, too unusual, too challenging, or as long as it doesn't come too fast, too frequently. We've gone from rotary to touch-tone phones, from brick-sized cell phones to flip phones to smart phones that can take and send pictures, provide directions, relay text messages and emails, and access the worldwide web.

The third approach is resistance. We prefer to stick with what's familiar and comfortable, and we especially resist personal change, the changes that bring meaningful growth. Changing the way we approach confrontational situations, the way we provide acknowledgement, the way we initiate contact with those we haven't met, the way we approach the adventuresome, the difficult—these are the kinds of changes needed to grow as an engaging leader.

Charged Up

This story by Arlen demonstrates what happens when a person initiates change:

> I had been taking inventory at our battery distribution center branch for more than a year. I not only did the inventory, I did all the ordering of the replacement batteries. After I completed the inventory and wrote up the orders, I always had to turn my work in to the president for his inspection and approval.
>
> One day, after gathering confidence from my class and pledging "never again will I be afraid to stand up, speak out, and be counted," I called the president of the company at corporate headquarters. We had a 10- to 15-minute conversation. I told him that I felt I had proven myself—that I wanted all the responsibility and, of course, accountability that appropriately goes with my job, including approving the orders I recommend. I wanted to inspect and be responsible and accountable for all of my work. Since I was closer to our seasonal demands and changing customer base, we would have fewer inventory "outs" and faster inventory turns. This would give us a greater return on investment and greater profits.
>
> I caught him off guard! He didn't know what to say. He said, "Let me think about it." When he called me back the next morning, he said, "It's all yours!" He even went on to say that he wished he had more employees

like me—people who would ask for additional responsibility and welcome the accountability that goes with the responsibility.

I have had this new expanded responsibility and challenge for two months. Everything is going great. I can't wait for review time to roll around.

The lesson I learned from this experience is when I concentrate on my abilities and take credit for what I have accomplished, all my achievements, it gives me the self-confidence to be assertive.

A Fish Story

What happens when we resist change? We get stuck! Whenever I feel myself resisting change, a little fish comes to mind:

For years I wanted an aquarium. One day my wife and I visited an antique store in Seattle, WA, and I spotted a used aquarium. It was complete in every detail, including an unusual custom-made enclosure cabinet. I admired it. On my birthday a few months later, to my amazement, there it was in my foyer when I walked in the door. My wife had bought it and had it shipped from Seattle to our home in Portland, OR. After a few weeks, we set it up in my office with what seemed to be the right fish and accessories, including a little sunken ship with a hole in the side where the fish could swim in and out and hide. One of the fish, which looked a lot like a flat sunfish but a little smaller, always seemed to hide inside the hull of the sunken model ship.

As days and weeks progressed, the fish grew. We commented, "Boy, it better be careful or it's going to get stuck in the little ship." Sure enough, a few weeks later I walked in the office on a Saturday and there it was trying to get out of the hull of the ship, stuck and flapping with all of its might. I reached down into the tank and tried to move the ship so the fish could get free, but it couldn't. It was really stuck. I shook the ship and the fish finally came free. I finished my work in the office, went home, and came back on Monday. To my disappointment, I found the little fish floating dead on top of the water.

This simple story illustrates what happens when you retreat to your comfort zone. You get "stuck" and it can be deadly. The walls of your comfort zone grow higher, thicker, and the chances of escape become less and less. You lose your self-direction. Most of our failures in life are inside, not outside, our comfort zone. Lab participant Joe Hernandez told us, "The failure is not in trying—the failure is in *not trying*." We stand on the cusp, imagine failure, and don't try at all. As a result, we end up, as Thoreau said, leading "lives of quiet desperation."

For many years, ABC's *Wide World of Sports* started its program with the phrase, "The thrill of victory and the agony of defeat." Most people never know the thrill of victory because they don't risk the agony of defeat. Instead, they lead lives of quiet desperation. You have to strap on skis and make the run, take the risk, to win the medal. Why do we cling to our comfort zones? We are looking for security and think that by staying inside we obtain security. In truth, real security in life comes from moving out of your comfort zone, experiencing all of life with its many risks, growing and securing our measure of success. You can learn inside your comfort zone, but all significant growth takes place outside.

> *"Life shrinks or expands*
> *in proportion to one's courage."*
> Anais Nin

Jumping out of Your Comfort Zone

Kurt, a Lab participant, was afraid of heights. He set a goal to conquer this fear, to literally jump outside of his comfort zone by going skydiving. So one Saturday, he found himself 4,200 feet up in the sky with the door to the plane open. As the other skydivers stepped out of the door onto the strut and let go, Kurt thought to himself, "I'm not going to make it." But he attacked his fear and jumped out of the plane. Four seconds later the parachute opened. He experienced an unprecedented feeling of exhilaration, a sense of power that comes when we face and defeat a fear.

I'm not saying you need to jump out of an airplane to embrace change successfully. I am recommending that you jump out of your comfort zone, run for the nearest comfort zone exit, and you will experience personal exhilaration. Others will be inspired by your example, and you will lead an inspired team.

Adrift

When my wife, Donna Lee, and I went to see the much-acclaimed movie *Gravity*, I wasn't sure what to expect. The previews I had seen made it look a little slow. Instead, it was one of the most gripping, engaging 3D movies I'd seen for a long time. Donna Lee said she held her breath for 90 minutes. We were aghast as we watched the astronauts float away from their space station into outer space completely detached from their tethers. It's hard to imagine anything more terrifying.

The movie reminded me of how I've endeavored to describe the role fear plays in our lives—our fear of change, our fear of doing new things that we are unsure of.

When I've asked groups over the years why we're afraid of trying new things, why we're afraid to step outside of our comfort zone, the answer I usually get is, "We are afraid of failure."

I've never believed this. After all, anything we tried to do for the first time that could be rewarding we didn't do that well: our first attempts to walk resulted in failure and falling down; our first attempt to ride a bicycle resulted in failure; our first attempt to swim, to do most anything new and unusual that was challenging, resulted in failure. So I maintain we are not afraid of failure.

What are we afraid of then? Understanding the answer to this question could change your life forever. We are afraid of the reaction of others if and when we fail. We are afraid of being laughed at, afraid of ridicule, afraid of criticism and belittlement. Our ultimate fear is the fear of rejection. We are afraid of everyone turning their backs on us and walking away, leaving us alone—the fear of banishment, the fear of being all alone as if we're drifting in outer space without a tether, the kind of stark terror we may have experienced when we were lost at the fair, the park, or the grocery store as a child.

Now as you read these ideas, you know that this is absurd: it's not logical to think we'll be abandoned! Fear is not based on logic; none of our fears are based on logic, and perhaps understanding that few, if any, of our fears are logical will help us make important changes. When we come to that place of setting aside our fears, of being truly fearless, we live a life of poise and true confidence. When we come to that place of knowing we are loved, valued, appreciated, and needed, we can relax, let down our guard, let go of our defensiveness. When we are secure in the knowledge that we are loved and accepted just as we are, with nothing to prove, we will be the most powerful people on earth.

Experiments with babies have shown there are two natural, unlearned fears: the fear of falling and the fear of loud noises. All other fears are learned from vivid experience or from what we have been told by others. We hear our parents or others talk about their fears and their failures. We think about them, we wonder about them, we begin preparing the groundwork for our fears. Before we know it, these fears take on meaning, are confirmed in our experience, and we make them our own.

You Can Dissolve Your Fears

You can actually overcome your fears, not with reason, but by taking action. Fears can make you an extraordinary person. Fears can drive you up and on and be responsible for making you the poised and confident person you wish to become. As you experience and study your fears, you will learn to understand them. As you take action, you will be on your way to a significantly expanded comfort zone, greater personal fulfillment, and a changed life. You will position yourself to be an engaging leader.

Many people are afraid to take risks. They never learn to swim because they were taught by overly concerned, well-meaning adults to be afraid of water. There are people who are afraid of heights, the dark, crowds, being alone, speaking in public, asking for help, and on and on, all because of an experience they have probably long forgotten. Such fears are inhibiting and prevent us from receiving promotions, achieving our goals, and making personal progress. Fears can cause a loss of communication, teamwork, relationships, intimacy, and happiness unless we do something about them.

Every great person who has accomplished much had fears. They have made their fears work for them. How did they do this? They followed a powerful three-step plan, the same plan I am urging you to follow:

1. They recognized and identified their fears. Identify your fears, pinpoint them, and make them specific, because this is how you harness the emotion into a positive, progressive direction.

2. They made a plan of action. You will see that only action dispels fear and turns what could be a liability into an asset. Your plan of action is all important. Remember, "To act is to conquer."[8] To conquer is to bring about change.

3. They celebrated progress. When you conquer a fear or make strides toward expanding your comfort zone, celebrate it with a trusted friend. Successfully managing change is easier with a friend who supports you. It was Ralph Waldo Emerson who said, "What I need is someone who make me do what I can."

Change is inevitable and constant. You can replace your inclination to resist change with an attitude of embracing change. Decide now: will you wait for change to happen to you, always reacting to new circumstances, or will you proactively act with courage and be a pioneer of change? Today is the day for you to act courageously. Change some small part of your life and the world for the better, and let the results speak for themselves.

> *"Growth demands a temporary surrender of security.*
> *If we don't change, we don't grow."*
> Gail Sheehy

危机

The symbols for *crisis* in Chinese are made up of these two words—they are pronounced *wei ji*. *Wei* means "danger, peril." And *ji* means "opportunity, crucial point." So literally *wei* plus *ji* equals "danger" plus "opportunity."

Imagine a group of 12-year-olds lined up at the deep end of a swimming pool. They don't know how to swim. These kids could have learned how to swim at summer camp or at the community center, but they played volleyball. I'm hiding around the corner; when you give me the signal, I run out and knock all ten of these kids into the deep end of the pool. What have we created for these kids? You know the answer: *crisis*. What are they going to do?

I have asked hundreds of audiences this question. The answer I hear is "sink or swim." The truth is very few of us learned to swim by being thrown in over our heads, and the 12-year-olds are probably not going to sink either. They will cough, hack, spit, grab hold of the side of the pool and pull themselves out, then look for sympathy and reprisal. Now what are my chances of getting these kids back to the pool anytime soon? Slim to none. To them the pool represents failure and fear. Some of them may never learn to swim!

Now let's change this up just a bit; another group of 12-year-olds lined up at the deep end of the pool. The only difference—they all know how to swim; they are good swimmers. You give me the signal; I run out and knock them into the pool. What have I created for these kids? You're right—I have created an opportunity for a game. What are they going to do? If there is a leader among them, they are going to get out of the pool, chase me down, and throw me in. What is the difference that resulted in such totally different outcomes? Advance preparation!

My job and yours is to prepare for what is just around the corner so that when circumstances inevitably change, we don't experience crisis and chaos. Instead, we move from opportunity to opportunity. What will determine whether we experience an opportunity or a crisis? Not the event. It is all about preparation. Today is the day to prepare yourself for the opportunities that lie ahead.

Actions for Engaging Leaders

- Lean all you can from everyone in your life, value their experience, and then adapt your approach.
- Work with your team to create the change needed for continuous improvement.
- Look out on the horizon and honestly ask yourself, "If I continue to head in this direction, will I end up where I want to be?"

- Focus on the positive things in your life; inventory your successes; count them up; then boldly look for opportunities to take on new challenges.

Benefits You Will Gain

- You will become a stronger leader and results in all key result areas will continue to improve.
- You will be happy with your future.
- Others will be inspired by your example; you will be an engaging leader.
- You will achieve your goals and have the trophies to prove it.

"Collaboration, it turns out, is not a gift from the gods but a skill that requires effort and practice."

Douglas B. Reeves

Synergistic Teamwork

Roger, maintenance foreman for a paper mill where we conducted an 18-month Continuous Improvement Program, said, "Larry, you have ruined *Star Trek* for me." He explained he could no longer watch the show with the detached enjoyment he was used to. Instead, he was noticing how the characters were working together—how they were conducting meetings and making decisions. He explained why:

The Turbo program opened my eyes to the changes I saw in *Star Trek*," he said, and described what he had learned about conducting team meetings. "We even learned that the arrangement of the room is important. The preferred arrangement, we learned, is in a circle, or a semicircle facing a flip chart. I noticed for the first time that when the crew of the new Enterprise is faced with a problem, Captain Picard calls everyone to the Ready Room, and his officers sit facing each other at a table in a circle. Everyone is invited to air their view of the problem and its causes, and to make suggestions for solving the problem and meeting the challenge. On the bridge of the new Enterprise, action assignments are made, and the command team sits on a horseshoe-shaped sofa, facing the main view screen.

The seating arrangement to be avoided is a group arrayed in front of and below the leader—the old Captain Kirk style. This is what made me realize that there has been a fundamental change in the management style of the United Federation of Planets.

The actual trigger was Larry's comment which compared the old style of management to Captain Horatio Hornblower, C.S. Forester's fictional character, who sailed the seas at a time when long-distance communication was nonexistent, and, except for a handful of officers, the crews were pressed into service. Navy ships were out of touch with civilization for months and even years at a time. Decisions could be made only by the captain, who commanded the ship with a lash—who could literally make a crewman walk the plank. A bit of little-known trivia is that Gene Roddenberry, the creator of *Star Trek*, as a youngster idolized Captain Hornblower and later used him as the model for the role of Captain James T. Kirk.

Now on Saturday evening instead of sitting back and enjoying *Star Trek*, old and new, I find myself picking them apart. Here's Captain Kirk, perched on his throne at the center of the bridge, the classic old-style boss from the '50s, confronted with a problem. He calls in Mr. Spock and Bones, the advisors he seems to most trust, and makes a vain attempt at consultative decision making before doing it his own way (command decision making), charging off and nearly getting killed in the process because it is "his job."

An hour later I'll be cringing while Jean Luc Picard, ever the efficient twenty-fifth-century manager, agonizes over some situation competently supported by Data, Number One, Facilitator Troy, Dr. Beverly, and her son Wesley. Eventually they'll probably decide to beam Worf down to the planet for some intelligence if the aliens haven't already died of boredom. At the end, everybody will have adjourned to Ten-Forward (Whoopi's place) to celebrate another small success in the conquest of outer space.

Command to Commitment

As Roger noticed watching *Star Trek,* there is a difference in the management style of today's leaders and their counterparts of years ago, moving from command-and-control decision making to a collaborative team approach to engagement. Engaging leaders seek innovative ideas from those closest to the work—a way of moving from command to commitment. This results in continually improving effective processes and creates engaged employees who have the authority to stop processes when errors in quality are observed. They feel welcome to present their ideas and solutions without fear of personal putdowns or ridicule.

How about you? Are you contributing to the creation of an empowered team that is included in all decisions that affect their work and fully engages every day?

> *"Our emerging workforce is not interested in command-and-control leadership. They don't want to do things because I said so; they want to do things because they want to do them."*
> Irene Rosenfeld

Team Attitude

Jerry, the senior project manager for one of Oregon's top ten contractors, told us,

A $33 million project for Hewlett-Packard in Corvallis, the largest contract our company had ever tackled, brought together a diverse group of people who are very strong in their own way of doing business. To bring this powerful group together, we needed help. We facilitated a Turbo Leadership Construction Partnering

Session to help break down the barriers to successful teamwork. At the session, you could have heard a pin drop when Larry said, "No one in this room can succeed without everyone in the room succeeding."

It hit us like a ton of bricks. The truth sank in: our success was dependent on everyone else's success. We were no longer a gang of unrelated organizations out to do what was best for our own company at the expense of others. I could see attitudes change right before my eyes. We're not competing with each other—we're on the same team. We must succeed together.

Here are the key attitudes engaging leaders encourage among team members:

My contributions are important to the team; my team members' contributions are important to me. Everyone brings a unique combination of talents to the team. I shouldn't undervalue my capacity to contribute or anyone else's. I need to speak up, and I need to listen.

I am willing to sacrifice. I'm here to engage in creating and implementing the team's vision instead of insisting on my own way, my own ideas, my own vision.

My team can count on me, and I can count on my team. We keep our agreements to one another. We cover each other's positions when necessary. I must be a championship player for my team to be a championship team.

We succeed together. My success depends on everyone else's success. When the team wins, I win.

Horsing Around

The fact that an organization is greater than the sum of its parts was demonstrated for me in an unforgettable way in a story I heard of a contest in a Canadian logging camp. It was a contest to see whose horse could pull the greatest amount of weight. All the local citizens were excited and the festivities were going strong. Most of them were wagering on their favorite horse. They were bragging, speculating, sizing up, and calculating. When all the dust cleared, the winning horse pulled slightly more than 9,000 pounds. The one that came in second pulled only a little less than 9,000 pounds. Then, in the post-contest excitement, someone asked the question: "How much do you suppose both those horses could pull together?"

Heads snapped, eyes sparkled, and after a sufficient amount of calculating, bets were put down again. Most of the bets were about 18,000 pounds as the maximum load the horses in tandem could pull together.

The horses were harnessed together, and they gave a mighty pull. When their load was measured, they had pulled 30,000 pounds! They proved that with engaged teamwork, you achieve *synergism*, and 9 + 9 = 30! Synergism comes from the Greek word *synergos*, which means "to work together." The English definition you may be familiar with is "the whole is greater than the sum of its parts." We all want to be part of something bigger than ourselves. We all want the energizing juice of experiencing synergism as part of a winning team.

"We = power."
Lorii Myers

Crew Team

Jim, the owner of a heating and air conditioning company in Seattle, told us,

While I was attending the University of Washington, I was a member of the rowing crew. When the team was pulling in unison, synchronized, our shell would literally rise from the water. It almost skimmed across Lake Union. For our crew to lose the synergetic effect of that extraordinary teamwork, only one team member had to be off pace. For the shell to have that lift, all team members had to pull on the oars with the same amount of stress at the exact same time.

One crew member pulling too early or too late can make the difference in any endeavor. Through training, team members learn to pull with the same amount of stress and to have the coordination to speed up at the right pace without losing their synchronization. It is the coxswain's job to call out the cadence so the team knows how and when to pull. The engaging leader is the coxswain, providing the guidance to ensure the cadence required to keep the team pulling together as the pace increases.

Good Team, Great Team

An advertisement by Signode Industries Inc. in *Business Week Magazine* describes a good team and a *great* team:

For the good team, each member holds the same vision.

The crew members want to be right where they are. They understand the risks, as well as the rewards. They know when difficulties present themselves, they must pull together.

The more experienced are willing to set the pace and lead by example.

But the great team?

You sense a unique harmony when the oars touch the water. The oarsmen carry a penetrating sense of purpose. There is an unspoken confidence. It is as if only this group, right now, is doing the task exactly this way, with a special rhythm and commitment.

Harmony. Purpose. Confidence. Commitment. This is the kind of focused teamwork you build by creating engagement.

Uncle Bill

My Uncle Bill Greer was one of the young men who stormed the cliffs of Normandy, France, on June 6, 1944: D-Day. After recovering for six months in a London Hospital, he returned home and bought a farm in Carter County, MO, with his mustering out pay.

In 1946, there was one thing you couldn't buy that we consider central to farming—a tractor. Unable to buy a tractor, my uncle did what his dad, my granddad, had done before him. He bought a team of mares and began to plow that old farm.

I was there one morning when he came in for lunch. My Aunt Ruth was cooking on their wood-burning cook stove. I was very young at the time, but I do clearly remember what he said: "When I go back out there this afternoon, I'm going to put Bess in the barn to rest, and I'm going to make Mabel do all the plowing." I think he swore, which is why the incident so indelibly stuck in my mind. It was his opinion that Bess had been doing all the straining on the harness during the morning plowing. He was attempting to teach the mare a lesson on what happens when you don't engage for the team's success.

I know nothing about training horses, though I know something about human beings: *We let up if we feel let down.* It's the job of the engaging leader to create a culture where all members of the team feel supported: no one feels "let down" and no one "lets up." Everyone is engaged and pulls their weight equally at the right time, in the right manner, heading in the right direction, resulting in the marvel of synergism.

Empowering Team Members for Teamwork

An important part of your work as an engaging leader is empowering team members through delegation and training. Don't just dump responsibility on them and set them up to fail. Train, train, train. Encourage them to ask for the authority and resources they need. Expect some bumps. When you empower your team, you can expect some "dumb" decisions. Work actively with your team members, help them test their ideas, and learn from the process. Remember: a group of people isn't automatically a team. Developing an authentically synergistic team takes the time and effort of an engaged leader.

A winning team is a team that comes alive when each member appreciates the transcending power of a unified force. Remember what happens when two horses are aligned and pulling together: they can pull three times more than each one individually. With synergism, $9 + 9 = 30$!

> *"None of us is as smart as all of us."*
> Ken Blanchard and Sheldon Bowles

Yes, That's My Job!

Engaged team members share responsibilities to achieve the synergistic effect, and it makes things run more smoothly. Here's an example: I showed up early for a Saturday morning workshop I was conducting at a Beaverton hotel. We had provided a diagram of our desired setup, so I was disappointed to find the meeting room wasn't set up correctly. I called catering. The person who answered seemed confused about my request. Housekeeping was nearby, so I walked over and asked for what I needed, which was clearly outside of housekeeping's normal area of service. No one said, "That's not our job." Their response was "Let's see what we can find." They found what we needed and, in a few quick moments, we got the meeting room set up correctly. Everything went smoothly, and the event was successful.

All of us must be willing to share one another's responsibilities if we are to have a winning team. If one person doesn't cover their own base, another person must cover it for them. You communicate this expectation to your team as well as demonstrate it by example. When we cover for each other, costs go down, performance goes up, the customer gets what they need, and everyone finds more meaning in their work. It's a winning experience.

New Idea

Lisa, corporate finance director for a commercial heating and air conditioning service contractor, told us that when a younger member of the company's operations department suggested a better way to manage purchase orders, her initial thought was "it will never work." Yet the younger team member had spent hours working with the cumbersome two-part purchase orders, tracking separate purchase order numbers. She was also imaginative and adept with technology. Lisa decided to listen. She told us,

> As I listened to her, I realized what a great idea she had! She created an Excel mail merge document where she logs a purchase order number, the customer name and agreement number, a system-generated work order number, and the cost. She then opens up a Word mail merge document that pulls the information from the Excel document and populates the necessary fields. This Word document now replaces the two-part purchase order we typically use, and can now be easily emailed from her desktop without having to be scanned into the computer first. The purchase orders are centrally stored electronically.
>
> I told her I thought her idea was great and asked her to do a "trial run" for her office before we launch it to the rest of our offices. Purchase orders for belts and filters for scheduled maintenance agreements in the month of December were generated in mid-November, sent to the vendors, then forwarded to accounts payable for payment. All signs point to a job very well done!

Lisa's story is a powerful example of the benefits of placing the responsibility for efficiency and cost-reduction—and the authority for decision making—at the level closest to the work.

This is "empowerment," and it's an essential part of creating an engaged team. In empowered organizations, people are constantly looking for ways to cut costs, improve efficiency, and eliminate waste.

While it's still possible to hire an expert to tell you how to manage your processes, we know that our work is continually evolving. We've never found the perfect way to organize our work, and we're constantly reorganizing. When processes are improved upstream in the work flow, it creates bottlenecks downstream. At that point, we have to reorganize the work downstream, and the people who do the work can be charged with the responsibility of continuing to improve the process. The leader's responsibility is to create an environment where people who do work feel empowered to study their processes and create ways of improving them. It's not a matter of command, control, and compliance; instead, we are fostering creativity, commitment, and cooperation.

As an engaging leader in your organization, a part of your responsibility is to find ways to empower team members to make cost-saving decisions. One way you can do this is by developing a recognition system that celebrates those who have made suggestions that are cost cutting, money saving, quality improving, or cycle shortening. Celebrate successes as a team.

In addition to recognition, it is important to reward in tangible ways those who help cut costs and improve efficiency. The ability to enlist the eager involvement of your team helps you qualify as an engaging leader. This kind of engaging leadership will help you maintain your market edge, help you enrich the lives of each member of your team, improve morale, decrease turnover, and win in a world that is increasingly competitive.

Golden Scraper

Team engagement and morale directly impacts quality and productivity. This was demonstrated while we were conducting a Performance Team Lab for a Wilsonville, OR, asphalt paving company. Sam, the superintendent, said,

> This past week in my front-line paving crew team meeting, I told the crew we were having a few problems with the density of our paving material. I explained in more detail than ever before our standards for thickness and edges. Their response was, "Thanks for including us. We can fix this.

As part of the meeting, Sam also presented his operator of the week with the "Golden Scraper Award," which he created to reward excellence and boost morale. Everyone loved it. Esprit de corps went up, production increased, and so did pride in their work. The crew, equipped with pertinent information about standards of performance, solved the density problem.

As I listened to Sam's report, I was reminded of the importance of including everyone who is part of the crew in the big picture. Never ask anyone to do anything unless you've shared the purpose of the task, how quality and performance are measured, how they can make the grade. At a recent Turbo event, one participant, explaining his need to ask questions and seek clarity on every project, said, *"I won't take a stand for anything I don't understand."* Help your team achieve synergistic teamwork by including every member in the big picture. Help them clearly understand the details and reasons behind it—the *what* and the *why*. The benefit you'll gain is an extraordinary increase in quality, production, and pride. This pride will help you and your team smoothly navigate difficult problems and make more profits.

Actions for Engaging Leaders

- Arrange meeting space in a way that encourages a team attitude.
- Set team goals, track progress, and celebrate successes.
- Train and cross train team members.
- Act as a resource and mentor for your team.

Benefits You Will Gain

- Team members will contribute ideas for improved processes.
- Your team will gain confidence and become more innovative.
- Your company will run more smoothly.
- Your customers will be impressed with your responsiveness.

>>>Part Two

---

15 Principles of Engaging Leadership

"Ideals are like stars; you will not succeed in touching them with your hands. But like the seafaring man on the desert of waters, you choose them as your guides, and following them you will reach your destiny."

Carl Schurz

>>>Principle 1

Lead from High Ideals

A project manager told us this story about upholding values in the face of budget pressures:

Three weeks ago, inspectors from the Washington Safety and Health Administration visited the job site at one of our projects. They issued several safety violations because we had not taken adequate fall protection precautions. This inspection came at a time when we were just starting a phase of the work that took place on upper levels in unprotected areas—the kind of work where fall protection needs to be employed.

Since it is the project superintendent's responsibility to run a safe project, I set up a meeting between myself, the project superintendent, and our safety coordinator to resolve the issue and clean up the problems. The superintendent's initial defensive response was, "There's not enough money in the budget for all these safety precautions. Besides, Washington State's rules are unrealistic anyway! We never have to do all that stuff in Oregon!"

So I decided to start the meeting using the process of positive correction. I started by pointing out how well the project had been progressing. I reminded everyone how complex the design was and the fact that the job was bid when the market was tight and we really needed the work. Because of this, we'd bid the job extra low.

I told them that we may not have included enough money in the budget for all the appropriate safety precautions. I then restated our unswerving commitment to safety. I told the superintendent that we would have a safe project even if we had cost overruns in this area. I committed to get all the current Washington State regulations to him within the next four days. He agreed to conform to the standards as prescribed by the state for running a safe job.

Today the work that requires fall protection is essentially complete, and we have received several compliments on a safe and clean project.

The lesson I learned is I can be direct. Using positive, professional communication that upholds our values is essential to obtaining the desired results.

True Value

Integrity is the most practical personal asset a leader can bring to an organization. You just have to look at the headlines to see the devastating consequences of managerial duplicity. When honesty is compromised at the top, an organization can be brought to its knees. *If you don't know what you stand for, you will fall for anything*. Engaging leaders know what their standards are and what they stand for. Engaging leaders have clarified their values and ideals. They remain true to ideals that have inspired and anchored them.

Enlightened leaders realize they must treasure the trust and respect of their team. They know trust and respect must be earned by leading from high ideals, by aligning actions with values, without compromise. They know they can lose trust and respect with one careless gesture, one thoughtless word.

The first step to securing the energetic engagement of your team is securing the full trust of everyone on your team. There are no shortcuts. Say what you mean. Mean what you say. Be reliable. Keep your agreements. Don't overstate your case. Never promise to do something you know you can't do or have no intention of doing. If you discover that you must break a commitment, communicate it quickly without blaming others. Engaging leaders have a reputation for being an example of keeping their word and living up to their commitments.

Dr. Melvin Sorcher, author of *Predicting Executive Success*, thinks that companies should ask these kinds of questions when judging the integrity of managers:

Does the individual

- provide backup to subordinates when they get in a jam, when subordinates take risks that don't pan out, or do they throw them under the bus?
- recognize and acknowledge their own personal failings?
- report progress toward objectives and organizational issues without spin, truthfully?
- refrain from backbiting behavior when their views differ from those of other departments?
- avoid treating company crises as opportunities to seize power or pin blame on others?[9]

Watch how people behave in situations that test their personal courage and commitment. Leaders who lead from high ideals always put the well-being of the people reporting to them above their own personal well-being.

How about you? Are you giving your team an example of the compelling values and high ideals you stand for?

Hosed

The importance of living up to our personal standards was brought home to me by David, who told us this story:

In the fall of 1973, I was standing on the fantail of a guided missile destroyer outside of San Diego, talking to second-class petty officer, Rubia. We were both looking with interest across the waterway at the dock where some crewmen from another ship were in the process of unloading some fire hoses that we knew had just passed hydrostatic testing. We looked at each other with smiles on our faces because we were thinking the same thing: "It would sure be nice to have those hoses on our ship."

It seemed to us that the chief engineer spent our entire budget on the main space repairs, and that there was no money left for accessories like the freshly tested fire hoses we were ogling. Now, there has always been a certain amount of thievery (sometimes called "scrounging") in the Navy. I guess that is a part of the adventure—scrounging was really quite commonplace. I said to Rubia, "Wouldn't it be nice to have those hoses?" and he said, "Yeah!"

I went back to my work station and began reassembling a spare pump I needed to finish repairing. About 15 minutes later, I was paged over the general announcing system: "Report to the chief engineer's stateroom immediately!"

I arrived at the chief engineer's stateroom as quickly as I could, knocked on his door, and announced my arrival. He invited me in and told me that Rubia had just been apprehended stealing fire hoses from the pier. My heart sank, my pulse increased. He went on to tell me that Rubia would probably go to the captain's mast, and then he told me how disappointed he was because Rubia had been such an outstanding leader.

I can't explain exactly how I felt, but I was very sick to my stomach. I was afraid to say anything, but after what seemed like ages I spoke up. I told the chief engineer that punishing Rubia was not necessary since I was the one who planted the idea in his head, so I should be the one held accountable for the whole incident. The chief engineer proceeded to give me the most professional chewing out I have ever received. He even questioned how I could be allowed to wear gold bars on my collar. As it turned out, Rubia was never disciplined.

The lesson I learned is that honesty and integrity are always the best policies, and that even if there is a tradition of questionable behavior—maybe especially if there is a history of questionable behavior—I must lead from high ideals.

> *"It is our choices that show what we truly are,*
> *far more than our abilities."*
>
> J.K. Rowling

In simple terms, moral principles are the guideposts that help us to differentiate between right and wrong. Engaging leaders must have a clearly defined set of guiding principles they are committed to as the basis for exercising leadership. The beliefs of a leader will obviously influence the actions they take. Beliefs are an individual's perception about the realities of the world in which they operate. In other words, our beliefs reflect how we think the world works.

Experiences in the real world can test our beliefs. As you mature, you must watch out for and critically evaluate any misalignment between your behaviors and your stated beliefs. As society continues to change and grow more complex, engaging leaders retain their bedrock values and apply them to today's challenges. We regard change that impacts us personally, that challenges our values, our view of the world and our place in it, with mixed emotions. Change forces us to examine our values and ideals.

All decisions, personal or business, are processed through our "personal value filter." The organization that has a strong sense of what is right will not do anything that is in conflict with these values under any circumstances.

When you have to act fast, you don't have time to stop and think things through. So you act from your heart and gut feelings—your spirit and intuition. This is where your values reside.

If the mission of your organization and the values of individuals are not in sync, it is essential to take time to resolve the issues, or individuals and the organization end up working at cross-purposes. This is why defining your values is so important.

When you define your organization's values, don't confuse what you are doing with "vision." Vision is your image of the future; values are the ethics which guide our journey. Values form the basis for the decisions the organization makes. Values are the golden rule for every organization. Values are practical things like operating within the law, valuing safety, and treating people fairly.

White Board Manager

When I read in the newspaper about a major shake-up at Jim's company, I called to see how he was doing. He said, "Well, I've got a real surprise for you." He told me he'd just been leap-frog promoted from an assistant to the plant manager position, managing over 85 people. We talked about how different the responsibility would be from his formal training as an engineer. At one point in the conversation he said, "The best manager I ever worked for was in a Hawaiian sugar plant. I've written his name on the white board in my office. No one knows what it means except me. Every time I look at his name, it reminds me to manage like he did."

I thought to myself, "Wow, I wonder if that Hawaiian manager knows what a difference he made in Jim's life." I wonder if anyone who ever worked for me would hold me up as a model manager. Is there anything more important, more powerful, or more meaningful that you can do with your life than to make others want to emulate you as the ideal? This leader made a life-changing difference in Jim, and now Jim wants to make a life-changing difference in the people on his team.

Each of us has an opportunity to make a lasting impact on others. As you assume the mantle of leadership, you have the opportunity to change others for the better.

So remember, your job is to do more than build widgets and make a profit. Your job is to build people and make them successful. Your job is to bring out the best in everyone—every person who works and lives with you, so they can realize their full potential. By doing this, you'll be realizing your greatest potential.

> *"Leadership is about making others better as a result of your presence and making sure that impact lasts in your absence."*
>
> Sheryl Sandberg

Your Legends

Years ago in a leadership class I was teaching, I heard two starkly contrasting stories—both took place almost 20 years earlier, though they were told as if they had happened yesterday! One was about the boss who fired our class member (who, at the time, was the delivery boy), after accusing him of stealing parts from his delivery truck. Our class member learned later the real reason he was fired: the boss wanted to give the delivery job to his nephew and didn't have the courage to tell the truth. The second was the story of the boss who loaned our class member $4,000 after his wife left him in the lurch.

Here it was, 20 years later, and these stories and the companies' reputations were still remembered. That's what is known as a legend, and legends play an important part in the creation of a culture. The question for you today is: What kinds of legends are you creating? What kinds of stories are people telling about you that will be told over and over and over—maybe for 20 years or more?

Actions for Engaging Leaders

- Lead from high ideals.
- Never compromise your standards.
- Be sure the standards that support your values are clear.

Benefits You Will Gain

- You'll earn respect.
- Your team will feel safe and secure.
- Your organization will earn a great reputation.

"Everyone's affairs, however little,
are important to themselves"
Samuel Johnson

>>>Principle 2

Become Genuinely Interested

The sales manager of a metropolitan newspaper received a phone call from a client who asked that the sales representative assigned to the account be replaced. Why did the client "fire" the sales representative?

The answer was that this salesperson had not shown sufficient interest in the client's business. "She doesn't understand our business and seems unable or unwilling to learn about our products and our customers' applications," said the upset advertiser.

The client had gone so far as to invent code names for their products just to make it easier for the account representative to remember the products and applications. Still, she didn't seem to make the effort to grasp it. It seemed to the client as though she didn't care about their products or their business.

I have heard complaints for decades about self-centered salespeople—they care only about the sale and are indifferent toward the client's needs. The situation just described is one of the most blatant examples of self-centered complacency I have ever heard.

As you might have guessed, the sales representative was removed from the account. To her credit, she admitted that the customer was right and vowed to fully commit herself to all future accounts—to get to know her clients, their business, and why and how their products and services are important.

One of the fundamental leadership principles used by engaging leaders in their pursuit of excellence is "Become *genuinely* interested in others." A balance of personal strength and a warmth that comes from genuine interest in others results in personal charisma and magnetism. As you lead from strength with the developed habit of caring for and about others, you become a dynamic, engaging leader.

> *"It is one of the most beautiful compensations*
> *of this life that no one can sincerely try to help*
> *another without helping themselves."*
> Ralph Waldo Emerson

Know Your Clients

Recently, I conducted the first session of our ten-week sales training program for a machine engineering firm in Portland, OR. A week before the program started, we toured one of the plants serviced by our new client. In other words, we found out first hand where our new client sells their services, what they sell, to whom it is sold, and what their customers like and dislike about our client's products and services. So when I conducted their first training session, I drew on 25 years' sales training experience and, more importantly, my knowledge of my client's business.

The lesson I learned, once again, is the importance of becoming genuinely interested in our clients, doing my research with due diligence, listening to them, knowing their needs and desires.

Toward Intimacy

Years ago we watched *The Doctor*, a movie starring William Hurt and based on the true experience of a physician who treated his patients (and, as it turned out, everyone else in his life) like objects. His rationale? If I get too close to my patients, I'll lose my objectivity and therefore my effectiveness. When he is diagnosed with throat cancer and goes through the indignities and abuses of being a patient himself, the ordeal of chemotherapy and surgery, he discovers that he lacks intimacy with everyone in his life, including his wife and son.

This movie reminded me that we all desire intimacy. The only way you can find the joy of intimacy is through risk and vulnerability, a part of becoming genuinely interested in others. Here's the paradox: when you drop your defenses, you find your true identity. To be an engaging leader, strive to recognize your fears, drop your defenses, and let your true individuality show through. By doing this, you'll experience a deeper connection with everyone around you.

Heart Hunches

Following through on an intuition, I called Judy, a long-time friend who had moved to Phoenix. When I asked how she was doing, she responded, "Things are kind of up and down."

I said, "How do you mean, 'up and down'?"

"Marlin passed out at work the other day. His office called *me*. I asked, 'Why didn't you called 911 and get him to the hospital?' I jumped in the car and rushed over to his office. By the time I got there, he had been revived. He said it was just indigestion. I insisted that he go to the hospital. Well, he had had a mild heart attack."

Judy was stoic through this whole story until she said, "His boss, whose office is in California, never did call us. He has our home phone number; he could have easily called us." Her voice broke. I listened and supported her the best I could.

I'm glad I followed my intuition and reached out, even though I didn't know exactly what to say. Follow your heart and hunches: you will prove to yourself that your gut feelings are often more reliable than your head. Reach out to everyone in your world with genuine interest, even when you're not sure what to say. Be willing to be vulnerable.

Talent Scout

Phil, owner of a steel erection company, told us he had a new iron worker on the job that he hadn't taken the time to get to know. He wanted to put the 15 Leadership Principles into practice and intuitively knew (as we all do) that the better we know a person, the more successfully we can work together. So, he built some "shoe-leather equity" by doing what we call an "inner-view." He began by asking the new crew member a few questions about his background and experience. Open-ended questions about former challenges and enjoyable work experiences allowed Phil to get an inner view.

To Phil's surprise, the crew member had been a foreman on similar jobs. At one time he had even owned his own construction company. Phil told us this fellow has a lot of great ideas that will streamline their projects. He never would have discovered the ideas, talent and ability if he hadn't gotten out of his office and shown genuine interest.

How about you? Who should you get to know better? Become a talent scout today: show genuine interest by conducting your own "inner-views."

Lunch Break

Red, superintendent for Oregon's largest highway contractor, told us he and one of his key office staff have entirely different work styles. Red is more deliberate, a little slower in making decisions, and may appear indecisive. His associate is quick to decide, maybe a little impulsive. Determined to improve their relationship, Red took her out to lunch and asked about her interests, successes, and goals. As it turned out, they actually had a lot in common.

When it was time to hire a new receptionist, Red had his ideas about the kind of person they needed, and his associate had hers. Red listened to her ideas, and the new receptionist she hired is great. Red has made it a point to brag to everyone about *her* decision. Red said, "It's much easier to have an engaged team when I express a genuine interest in all of my players."

Becoming genuinely interested in others enables us to find out who they are and who they would like to be. Knowing what their desires, motivations, goals, and ideals are puts us in a far better position to win their engagement, to lead successfully, *to bring out the best so results exceed high expectations.*

Engaging leaders work with others according to their preferences and personalities. By showing people that you know who they are and that you respect them, you demonstrate genuine interest. Make full use of the small points you know about the people you work with. Show them you know how they feel and what matters to them.

Engaging leaders strive to build personal relationships with their teams. When you establish relationships with your employees, you build trust and they feel valued. Valued employees engage and get the job done right. Conversely, employees who feel a lack of connection become disengaged. They underperform, leave, or, worse, stagnate. Let's remember that people quit people, not companies.

See Them at Their Best

I attended a seminar conducted by Dr. Rick Brinkman, a long-time friend of mine. As Mastermind partners, we've shared highlights, set goals, and celebrated successes hundreds of times. As I watched him make a brilliant presentation, I realized I didn't really know him. I had described him to myself in ways that were limiting and inadequate. Even now, I can't describe his capabilities and strengths as fully as he deserves. The lesson I learned from this experience is there is more excellence and potential inside each of us than meets the eye.

Take time to see those in your life perform at their best. When you see them at their best—whether making salsa, running a drill press, catching a grounder, or negotiating a change order—you may become aware of how remarkable they are. Greater awareness of your team's strengths will help you create synergistic alignment and attain full engagement.

Advancement

Showing genuine interest can help change negative attitudes. Jan told us,

> I had a problem with Irene for the last three years. She really resented my being promoted to supervisor of the accounting department. She had been employed with our firm for several years before I joined the company and she expected the promotion herself.
>
> In the last few weeks, I have stopped by her desk every day to see how she is doing and to find out what her main concerns are. I listen to what she says and doesn't say. I've made a point of writing her notes about the things she does well. I've tried to put myself in her shoes and treat her like I want to be treated.
>
> I can see a definite improvement in her work and, more importantly, in her attitude. She still doesn't like me being her supervisor, but she feels a lot better about herself and about me. She even said "thank you' in a note she left on my desk.

What can you learn from this simple story? People have feelings, whether you agree with them or not. You can sit in judgment and say, "She's a jerk," or accept responsibility as an engaging leader to help change those attitudes. Reread the above example. Look at the situation: it could have been a stalemate and considered impossible. But Jan accepted her responsibility as a leader to influence performance by showing genuine interest and taking a step back from her need to be "the boss" and always in control.

How about you? Is there a tough person in your life who needs your help in changing their attitude, someone whose respect and engagement you need? Here is the paradox—to gain people's respect, you begin by understanding and engaging their desire to feel important. You earn their respect by expressing your genuine interest in them.

Communication

You like to be in on things. You like your supervisors to take you into their confidence and keep you informed. When they don't, it makes you feel unimportant and your engagement can wane. So why should the people who work for you feel any different?

Engaging leaders show genuine interest in their team by empathizing with their desire to be informed, especially when changes occur. It's an important part of your job, so take it seriously and do it well. You know that when information stops, rumors start. You want cooperation and engagement, not just compliance. Keeping everyone well informed is an essential way to show genuine interest.

You've heard it said, "They don't care how much you know until they know how much you care." Not only are people the most important asset of your business, they are also the most variable asset: they have emotions, ups and downs. Performance above and beyond the call of duty seldom occurs unless you care about your team as individuals. In a tight labor market, your ability to attract and keep good people is vital to your success. The more talented members of your team expect to be treated with interest, courtesy, and respect, and it's in your best interest to do so. Those who seem less talented may expect less, yet when you take a genuine interest in them, they will grow in value to your team.

Count Down

Leslie, assistant manager for a restaurant chain in Yakima, WA, gave us an example of what genuine interest in a struggling employee can accomplish:

We were in the middle of a busy shift change and I needed a cashier who had worked for us for about six months to count down her till. I sent her to the office. Ten minutes later, she was still in there counting, a process that should take five minutes at most. I could feel my frustration growing and my temperature rising. I started thinking things like "How long does it take? Why can't she get this? She's been here long enough to know this."

Even though I was very busy, I went to check on her and see what the problem was. She said, "I can't get the drawer to the right starting amount."

I almost said something I would have regretted. Instead, I thought about the Leadership Principles that might help this situation. I stopped, took a deep breath, and said, "Let me show you how." I counted down her till the correct way while she watched me. I explained each step. Then I put the money back in the till and asked her to count it down as I talked her through it. That worked well, so I asked her to count down the till while explaining each step to me. This took less than ten minutes, and we counted the till three times.

When she was done with the last count, she looked at me with a great big smile and said, "Why didn't anyone show me this before? It was so easy!"

I felt good. I probably saved all the managers in the store from some frustration in the future. I am proud to say she is counting her tills much faster and doing it correctly every time.

The lesson I learned from this experience is when I show genuine interest by investing time in a struggling employee, it will save a lot of time and frustration in the future.

The objectives and goals of your organization, your team, must come first, and everyone, including those reporting to you, must recognize this. Becoming genuinely interested in your team members is not a conflicting goal. Far from it! When you show genuine interest, you strengthen your team and maximize their ability to reach your organization's objectives and goals. Do everything you can to show genuine interest in your team members. You will engage your team and know the joy of true leadership.

You can have technical skills, you can have all of the knowledge you need, you can be highly motivated and enthusiastic, but if you lack the people skills needed, you lose opportunities. As you become genuinely interested in everyone in your life, you strengthen your people skills and become an engaging leader.

> *"Kindness is irresistible, be it but sincere and*
> *no mock smile or mask assumed. For what*
> *can the most unconscionable of men do to thee*
> *if thou persist in being kindly to him?"*
>
> Marcus Aurelius

Actions for Engaging Leaders

- Redouble your commitment to knowing all of your customers (both internal and external customers).
- Keep everyone on your team well-informed.
- Show genuine interest in the people you lead.

Benefits You Will Gain

- You'll gain a greater sense of personal pride and self-respect.
- Your employees will be happier and more productive.
- You will build an engaged championship team.

*"Any fool can criticize, condemn and complain –
and most fools do."*

Benjamin Franklin

>>>Principle 3

Don't Criticize, Condemn, or Complain

At about 10 p.m., armed with flashlights, pick and shovel, Loren (our youngest son) and I set out to solve the problem that had been bothering us all summer—yellow jackets landing on our food while we were trying to eat out on the deck. We began to dig in the area where the yellow jackets seemed to be coming from. We dug down about three feet when we heard *buzz-buzz-buzz*. Yikes! I felt a bee on my forehead. I yelled. Loren yelled. We ran as fast as we could for the back door of the house. Several stings later, we were safe inside.

What the yellow jackets did was perfectly natural: they defended themselves. They successfully protected their home, their turf, their territory. You and I may be more like yellow jackets than we realize. When you feel you are being attacked, the most natural thing to do is fight back. Think twice before you attack anyone with criticism.

Criticism fixes blame on the person who did something "wrong." Criticism questions the competence or character of a person instead of focusing attention on performance. It is demoralizing and disempowering. The result is resentment because it hurts a person's sense of pride. You will never secure engagement if people feel you are their critic.

Criticism is often an unconscious habit. You may subconsciously believe people will take advantage of you if you don't criticize. Our own uncertainties can make us more defensive and critical.

Criticism results in people striving to justify themselves. It cuts off communication, reduces engagement, dampens enthusiasm and creativity, and diminishes job satisfaction. Criticism causes the receiver to feel instead of listen. It sabotages a positive working environment.

Have You Noticed?

Mike discovered the effects of criticism on his environment the hard way. He had been trying to get two team members to work more cooperatively together. They didn't communicate civilly or show signs of cooperation.

One day as he was heading downstairs, he was surprised to hear the voices of his two uncooperative team members. He slowed his pace, curious to hear what they were talking about. He didn't like what he heard:

"Mike is our biggest problem around here."

"You're not kidding. All he does when he comes into our area is criticize. First thing he says is, 'Have you noticed . . .' followed by something he wants me to change, some piddly, insignificant thing. He never says he's noticed improvements, progress, or gains."

The other person responded, "It's a joke in our department. Everybody looks at each other when he says, 'Have you noticed . . .' because we know some kind of criticism is just around the corner."

Mike quietly walked back up the stairs with something to think about.

That night, when he got home, he asked his wife, "Do I ever notice things around here?"

She said, "Do you ever notice things around here? That's all you ever do is notice things around here!"

Fortunately for Mike (and his marriage), those two coworkers helped him see his unconscious habit of continually criticizing. It had become such an ingrained behavior that Mike was totally unaware of it.

Empty

Larry, purchasing manager for a barge manufacturer, learned that even joking criticism can be harmful:

> In the 1970s, we were in the throes of a nationwide gasoline shortage. I was working for Gunderson down on Front Street. As I look back, I must admit I made myself the resident pain in the butt. I mercilessly teased anyone who made the mistake of running out of gas, especially if they got stranded. I accused them of only using the top half of their gas tank and any other jabs I could think of to hassle or embarrass them.
>
> Well, as fate would have it, I was running a lunchtime errand down on St. Helens Road when my car started to cough and gasp. The resident "pain in the butt" had just run out of gas. I was way out of town, and I knew there were no gas stations for miles around. I called the garage at work and asked them to quietly bring me a can of gasoline. Unbeknownst to me, they called one of my coworkers and ask him to drive the gas out to me. Once my fellow employees were alerted to my peril, my worst nightmare happened. There were signs and banners everywhere announcing that Larry had run out of gas. And, of course, the supply of jibes about fate seemed unending.
>
> Later on that evening, I was telling my story to a friend. She said, "I thought you had AAA road service.

Wouldn't they have brought you a can of gas?"

I'm sure they would have if I had thought to call them. Now I had double egg on my face.

The lesson I learned from this experience is to withhold judgment, to allow others the same room for error I want when I screw up. I learned the absurdity of expecting others to be perfect. This lesson forcefully reminded me of the fact that others will judge with the same harshness or patience as I use with them.

Yes, criticism is like a boomerang: it comes back and sometimes catches you in the backside. Remember: jibes that may seem like teasing to you can feel like stinging criticism to others.

Critic's Vacation

A few minutes into my meeting with a young first-level manager scheduled to start the Leadership Development Lab, I said, "You've got a pretty active 'critic.' You'll need to leave your critic outside the classroom if you're going to gain full value from the experience."

He responded, "You're very insightful. I do have an active critic."

Truth be told, most of us do. If you want to experience a lift, let your critic take a vacation or better yet, a leave of absence. Give your critic—that part of your personality that tends to scrutinize and criticize—a vacation. Stop trying to right the world, to fix everything and everyone. You may be amazed at how much renewed energy and fun you'll have. Giving your critic a few weeks off will help you create higher levels of engagement and could result in your team fully showing up for work!

Criticizing Diminishes Teams

John told us about the effects of criticism on his son's little-league team:

The head coach was a perfectionist, demanding that all of the boys play like men. He criticized any mistake, lost his temper regularly, and, finally, after a losing game, told the boys that they were "losers" and quit. This left me and another inexperienced father to coach the team for the rest of the season. We were in last place. We began to encourage the team. By the end of the season, we were number six in the league and made the playoffs. It didn't stop there. We won the first playoff game, then the second, and beat all the teams who'd beaten us earlier in the season. You guessed it—we took first place in our league.

The lesson we can learn from John's story is that criticizing diminishes teamwork; it actually holds teams back, disempowers, and robs people of their strengths.

> *"Don't judge any man until you have walked two moons in his moccasins."*
>
> American Indian proverb

Condemning

Condemning may be more harmful than criticizing. Criticizing is expressing disapproval *to* someone; condemning is saying something negative *about* someone—pointing out their faults to others. Talking behind people's backs borders on immorality and is demoralizing to the speaker and the listener. Other people may be totally wrong, but they usually don't think so! Do not condemn them. Instead, try to understand them. Too often we condemn because we don't have the courage to confront, to go direct, to say, "Can I talk with you?

Inspector

Jeff, president of a custom alloy metal fabricating company, told us what he learned about condemning:

John, an inspector for one of my customers, liked to tell everyone how to do their job, making him seem like a real know-it-all. We were working on a six-month-long project and struggled with the feeling that we could never quite measure up to John's expectations. The job was becoming a real pain. I began joking about John's manner of "helping" with one of John's coworkers. We both agreed he was a real "ass" to work with.

About two months after completing the job, I was supervising the installation of one of our tanks on another project. I overheard some of the engineers from John's company talking, and someone said one of the other inspectors was acting a lot like John. Without thinking, I said in a joking manner, "What—you mean acting like an ass?" The whole place went quiet. I knew I had put my foot in my mouth. I felt awkward, to say the least. I did my best to make a joke out of it.

About six weeks later, I received a call from John who said, "Hello, this is your favorite ass." Because of my mistake, there are real problems in our relationship. I am still struggling to get John's final approval on the completion of one of our jobs. The lesson I learned from this experience is never speak critically about someone behind their back. Even if I'm making a joke out of it, it will backfire!

> *"Nine in ten of every company you are with will avail themselves of every indiscreet and unguarded expression of yours if they can turn it to their own advantage."*
>
> Lord Chesterfield

Lipstick Mafia

There's always more to people than what meets the eye. Amity, bookkeeper for a marketing company in Yakima, WA, learned this when she glibly labeled her competitors at a race:

A year ago, I participated in the Gap-to-Gap Relay Race. At the starting line, I sized up my competition. As I looked around, I noticed an older gentleman in his 70s. I was pretty confident I could beat him. On my left was a young girl with pink bunny ears on her head, the kind you see on Playboy models. I guess this was her metaphor for being fast. I spotted another younger woman with her hair all done fancy and loads of makeup. I couldn't quite figure out how to interpret her appearance.

The gun went off and I easily passed the older man. Next in my sights was the "lipstick mafia" woman. I finally passed her around the halfway mark and put all my effort in chasing down "bunny ears." I never did catch her, but still felt like I had won by passing two of my "chosen" competition. Later that evening, I was telling friends about how I beat "lipstick mafia." One of my dinner companions worked with her and told me she was three months pregnant! Boy, was I embarrassed!

The lesson I learned from this experience is to never judge a person by their makeup or outward appearance. Give people the benefit of the doubt; expect that they have more potential than may be apparent on the surface. You may be pleasantly surprised.

This story reminds us how important it is to be careful about judging people. There is always more to the story than meets the eye. Take a closer, deeper look. You will be amazed at what you discover.

"Do not judge and you will never be mistaken."
Rousseau

Mother's Day

Sunday, after church, our son took us out for Mother's Day lunch. The line was backed up. We waited and waited. The manager looked at us and said, in a sort of critical, demeaning way, "She's new," pointing at the girl who was supposed to take our order.

Like criticizing, condemning can arise from our own insecurities. Our server's manager, who was belittling and condemning her, was trying to turn the focus away from himself and his responsibility to properly train her. His remark didn't help her, and it made him look bad as well.

The lesson I learned from this experience is the importance of never condemning another member of my team *publicly*. We resolve our differences and conflicts behind closed doors. To the outside world, we present a united front: we speak with one voice, with no minority reports. Resolve to be open with your team, to allow for feedback and coaching, and to never speak critically of a fellow team member to the outside world.

Just the Facts

Sometimes it seems as though you are being *invited* to condemn someone. A department supervisor for a Northwest healthcare organization told us about such a time:

> My physician partner is extremely intelligent, but his time management, or lack of it, was resulting in failed promises and broken appointments. His lack of punctuality affected customer service and our department's morale. I had lost all respect for him because of his disrespectful treatment of others.
>
> This situation had degenerated to the point that he was called in for a formal review with the executive board to discuss customer complaints and his impact on employee morale. They adjourned the meeting with a corrective action plan, set specific goals for him, and scheduled a six-month follow-up.
>
> About a week before the follow-up meeting, I received a call from the chairman of the board asking for a frank update on how the doctor had been doing. I had noticed a small improvement in his time management,

but had also started to notice a few other areas that were slipping. I had plenty of ammunition to "throw him under the bus." After gathering my thoughts, I wrote an objective report that I was proud to provide to the board. I stated only the facts and kept all emotional, personal, and staff frustration out of it. I supplied various forms of documentation and never said one critical word in my half-page report.

The lesson I learned from this experience is that I can state the truth, whether positive or negative, without putting my own personal spin or emotion into it.

Sometimes we do need to relay negative information about a team member's performance through appropriate channels. Take the time to edit your anger out.

Complaining

Tom told us a great story about complaining:

After memorizing Turbo's 15 Leadership Principles, making them a permanent part of my brain, I took them home. My first challenge occurred soon after I walked in the back door. I needed to relearn thinking and speaking if I was going to communicate with my wife without violating principle number three—Don't Criticize, Condemn, or Complain. No more complaining required impromptu, innovative thinking to organize my thoughts in a new, totally positive manner.

For years, I've been trying to get my wife to leave the catsup out of the refrigerator. I like it warm. All my complaining to her about it has gone unheeded because the catsup is still kept in the refrigerator. The lesson I learned is that complaining in any form is not effective.

Complaining is not only ineffective; it takes the sweetness out of life and relationships. Who wants to be around the dull-minded, negative speck spotter who sees and points out the little imperfections that always exist?

Too hot, too cold, too fast, too slow, too big, too little, too short, too tall, too dry, too wet, too skinny, too fat—one of the ways you can distinguish yourself from others is by refraining from complaining with uncomplimentary adjectives.

Email

Elbert Hubbard had some good advice:

It is foolish to say sharp, hasty things, but it is a great deal more foolish to write 'm. When a man sends you an impudent letter, sit right down and give it back to him with interest ten times compounded—and then throw both letters in the wastebasket.[10]

Elbert Hubbard penned these words nearly 100 years ago. His advice seems more needed today than ever. There are text messages and emails flying around that are critical, harsh, and hurtful. *Never* send an email that employs any one of the 3 C's! If you are on the receiving end of a 3-C email chain, sit down, write your response, then hit "Delete."

Am I builder who works with care,
measuring life by the rule and square?
Am I shaping my deeds to a well-made plan
patiently doing the best I can?
Or am I wrecker, who walks the town
content with the labor of tearing down?

Author Unknown

A Better Way

Replace criticizing, condemning, and complaining with encouragement, coaching, and correcting. Focus on bringing forth each person's excellence so that the job gets done, not judging the individual when their performance is less than perfect. When done properly, the conversation about what isn't working moves the work forward and secures engagement.

Mark, a foreman for a Clark County commercial plumbing contractor, told us about trying a new approach with his son:

When we were asked to choose someone we wanted to improve our relationship with, I chose my oldest son. For the past several years, our relationship has been strained. I wanted to coach him to be a better student and athlete, to grow into a successful young man.

At Session 3, I realized for the first time that I wasn't competently "coaching"; instead, I was clumsily criticizing. I would give him praise, and then I would say the dreaded B-word: "but." I realized for the first time that as soon as I said "but," he would shut down entirely and quit listening. It wouldn't matter if I was giving him the greatest advice in the world—he would refuse to listen as soon as the negative "but" came out of my mouth. I had become furious with him for not listening, and he kept getting mad at me because I was criticizing him. It was a vicious, downward cycle.

Then I began to implement the 4 P's of Empowering Coaching (see next page) in place of the dreaded "but." Replacing the 3 C's with the 4 P's has led to us having a much improved relationship. He no longer shuts me out, and I'm no longer mad at him for not listening. What's more, he implements the advice I give him.

The lesson I learned from this experience is that criticism comes naturally; I do it unintentionally. I must be fully conscious to provide constructive feedback.

The 4 P's of Empowering Coaching

1. **Praise:** Tell them what they are doing well.
2. **Permission:** Ask permission to provide input.
3. **Performance:** Show them one way to improve; focus on behavior.
4. **Prediction:** Predict successful and practical outcomes.

Actions for Engaging Leaders

- Stop being petty about things that really don't matter.
- Express your thoughts in positive terms.
- Focus on empowering coaching instead of the dreaded "but" of criticism.

Benefits You Will Gain

- The responses to your interactions will be positive.
- You will live in a more harmonious world.
- You will become an empowering coach.

"The deepest principle of human nature
is the craving to be appreciated."
William James

>>>Principle 4

Provide Acknowledgement

Not long ago I had a cup of coffee with George, a 52-year-old district manager who is responsible for 13 stores of a major food retail chain. He has been with the company for almost 20 years. When George took over his current district, it was losing $500,000 per year. For the past three years, under his leadership, the territory has averaged a profit of $2,000,000 per year.

George was recently told that he would have to be happy with his current job for the balance of his career. In other words, he has been shelved. Surprisingly, George's complaint about the company wasn't that he's been shelved. His complaint was that he hasn't received any recognition for taking his district from losses to profits. He felt that the only interaction he had with senior management focused on what wasn't right, what needed to be fixed.

I have found that regardless of the level in an organization, the lack of recognition is one of the most common complaints. Acknowledging individuals' contributions will increase the effectiveness of all your efforts.

In the past, organizations treated people as if they were wage slaves. Workers who punched a clock and were paid by the hour were regarded as units of production. The individual's desires, interests, dreams, and hopes were of little importance to the enterprise. Workers were supposed to check invoices, operate a winder, or place rivets in an assembly as if they were machines. If you expected a pat on the back or credit for a job well done, you might be discarded for workers who performed their jobs by rote and never complained or required recognition.

Today engaging leaders recognize that part of their job is to create an atmosphere that builds people. You create an atmosphere that builds people, brings out the best in people, by practicing the four steps of engaging acknowledgement. Most of us are not in the habit of giving acknowledgement. We all tend to take each other for granted. Your acknowledgement brings out the best in others by helping them believe in themselves and aim higher.

The four steps of engaging acknowledgement are paying positive attention, giving encouraging approval, expressing heartfelt appreciation, and offering insightful praise.

The Note

The division president of a major retailer with over 20,000 employees showed me, with great pride, a handwritten note he had recently received from the president of the company. It was a note of encouragement, recognition, and appreciation. These men had worked together for almost 30 years, and they obviously knew each other well. This division president deeply appreciated having tangible evidence that he was appreciated, not just taken for granted.

We all respond to acknowledgement. Our personal pride and self-confidence grows and our effectiveness increases when we receive meaningful acknowledgement.

"I will speak ill of no man
and speak all the good I know of everybody."
Benjamin Franklin

First Base: Pay Positive Attention

"Pay attention for showing up."

You want to hit a homerun with an engaged team. If you want people to accept your approval, start by paying attention. Giving approval to someone you haven't paid attention to is like skipping first base entirely and running directly to second base. People may reject your approval and appreciation when you have not earned the right by first paying positive attention. Effective attention is accomplished through warmly acknowledging others' presence. Say "Good morning. How are you doing?" Pay attention to people for showing up. They earn positive attention for being on time, dressed, and ready to play.

Pay Day

Kevin shared a fabulous story about the power of paying positive attention. He was finding it difficult to get full engagement from electricians called from the IBEW (International Brotherhood of Electrical Workers) hall. To solve his problem, Kevin began to practice the principle of paying positive attention—learning the electricians' names and then greeting them by name each morning. On payday, instead of the perfunctory process of placing checks in the paycheck slot, he made it a point to pass them out personally, including a note of thanks on each check. Kevin said the practice hasn't solved all of his motivation problems, but he's noticed a surprising improvement in engagement.

Ivory Tower

Recently we conducted the Leadership Development Lab for 30 supervisors of a pump manufacturer that employs over 250 people in their local plant. The company was facing major morale problems, and the plant was losing money. The first time I visited the corporate office and talked with the human resource director, he told me the president did not want to visit the company's local plant just across the parking lot from the corporate office because he was afraid it might show preferential treatment. He also avoided the plants in Louisiana, Toronto, and Vancouver because he feared they might think he was showing favoritism.

Six months after the completion of the LDL, the plant manager asked me to conduct a follow-up session for some of the supervisors who had participated. The personnel manager told me to expect six or eight people. Over twenty showed up. He had to drag in a lot of extra chairs. The supervisors told me, in a tone of surprise and disbelief, that the president had come out of his "ivory tower" to visit the plant floor, shaking hands and talking with the workers. His attention had a decidedly positive impact on morale.

Walk-About Leadership

A while back, I sat across from Bill, the president of a wholesale tool distributor in the greater Portland area. Their sales have gone from $6 million to more than $28 million in the last seven years. When I asked Bill how he did it, he said, "Well, I'm not a very good decision-maker anymore. I don't get a chance to make many decisions."

"So what do you do with your time?" someone asked.

He said, "I spend a lot of my time wandering around and talking with our people, asking them how I'm doing and how the company's doing, and what we can do to make their job easier. I may not be making a lot of decisions anymore, but I'm a lot smarter since I started managing by walking about."

Bill has actually made the most important decision leaders can make: the decision to pay attention to and empower their team by moving decisions to the front line.

How about you? Do you need to have your finger in every pie, to micromanage every decision? Today would be a great day to release a little. Pay more attention by walking about and asking others how *you're* doing instead of telling them how *they're* doing. You may be astounded at the engaging impact of your decision to pay attention.

On the Floor

Jim, operating assistant for a paper mill in northern Ontario, Canada, reported,

> When I made the commitment to be five times more enthusiastic about a project, I decided to spend five times more time on the floor, paying attention to the operators and millwrights in the maintenance group. I wanted to learn more about their ideas and concerns. I was determined to keep every conversation upbeat and positive, to focus on solutions and progress, not problems and setbacks. I wanted to be a non-defensive sounding board for their struggles with some of the changes they've had to make.

> As I explained the need for change and our machine's goal of 388 tpd (tons per day) in '08, I was amazed to find that some of the crew were unaware of our 388 goal. I put signs up all over the department (*388 in '08*). The feedback was positive and my increased presence on the floor was appreciated. My five times walk-about effort resulted in everyone being much better informed and understanding the importance of PM5's goal of *388 in '08*.

> The lesson I learned from this experience is never to assume that everyone in my department knows and understands the department's goals. It all happens on the floor, so I need to pay more attention to all of our crews.

Second Base: Give Encouraging Approval

"Give approval for being approximately right!"

Approval is acknowledging effort with acceptance and encouragement. For example, "You did well," "Keep it up,"

"That's the way." Your team earns approval for their engaged effort, not for being perfect.

Approval is effective when the receiver accepts it and feels encouraged. You must carefully observe to make sure the receiver accepts your approval. Remember: you earn the right to give approval by first paying positive attention.

Social Butterfly

Bob had a "social butterfly" on his crew who was not getting his job done. Bob decided to get to know the operator better. He started his campaign by paying attention and giving approval at every opportunity—any time the operator was performing a task even approximately right. A few days into his campaign, Bob had the weekend off. On the morning of his second day off, his phone rang. It was his weekend supervisor, Bruce, who said, "What have you done? I can't believe the change in our social butterfly!" The "social butterfly" had worked thirteen sets instead of his usual eight, a 62 percent increase in productivity, setting a new personal best for himself. This operator has since exceeded his personal best three more times.

Engaging leaders have learned to pay positive attention and always provide approval for every improvement, even the slightest improvement. Too often we feel we should not give approval for doing things "approximately right." We think it's enough that people are paid for doing their job. We tend to look for perfection. We focus on the blemish, the little flaw. We feel that by drawing attention to the imperfect, we will get improved performance. Instead, we breed resentment and dissatisfaction; our team is demoralized and disempowered. So instead of drawing attention to every little mistake, draw attention to every little improvement, even the slightest improvement.

Many of the people we live and work with have a lack of confidence. Effective approval helps build self-confidence and courage, and, in the process, improves performance. A pat on the back, though only a few vertebrae removed from a kick in the pants, is miles ahead in results.

Overdrive

Patrick, manager of an automotive repair shop, saw the difference giving approval can make. He told us,

> We hired a young man about a year ago. He's kind of a tall, skinny, bashful kid. It was my job to train him in the way we do things, including the way we inspect cars. After a couple of weeks, I showed him how to write up estimates. He just shuffled along. I let him work at his pace for a while to fully observe how he did things. I noticed that in many areas, he had a lot of technical knowledge that some of us lacked. He just didn't seem to have any "fire."
>
> One day when he came shuffling in, I asked him if he had a minute to talk. We weren't very busy that morning, so I took him off to the side and said, "Jaman, I admire your technical knowledge and the way you share it with us. You can walk by and look at the front or rear end of a truck and tell all its specs, including its gear ratios. That's amazing. This knowledge can make you as valuable to us as any senior technician." He smiled, turned a little red, and said, "Thank you." I felt I had unintentionally embarrassed him a little bit.
>
> At the end of the day, I told him he'd done a good job and I'd see him in the morning. The next day he was moving faster and working more quickly. He was more confident and friendly. I thought, "What's going on? This is a good thing." He had a productive day and he's been doing well ever since. It was great to see what a difference a few encouraging words could make.
>
> The lesson I learned from this experience is that when I provide encouraging approval to my team members, sometimes I can find an employee who is just as

valuable as someone who has been here for many years. Approval and encouragement are as important as paying them money because it gives their ego, their self-confidence, a boost, creating a more confident, productive team member.

Third Base: Give Heartfelt Appreciation!

"Give appreciation for going the extra mile."

A definition of "appreciate" is *"to recognize gratefully."*[11] Appreciation is expressed for discretionary effort, for going the extra mile: "Thank you for coming in early; I appreciate your putting in extra effort." If they don't accept your appreciation, go back to first base: start paying positive attention.

Turnover

One of the most pressing problems businesses face is high turnover. We remind clients, "People don't turn over. Often they just go down the street and interview a new boss."

Greg, who owns several McDonald's restaurants, made a decision to do something about the unsatisfactory turnover rate they were experiencing. Part of his program involved intensive leadership training for his supervisors, including helping them learn the importance of paying positive attention, giving approval for the slightest improvement, and giving lots of appreciation for extra effort. Greg began to chart his stores' employee turnover rate. After the leadership skills training, his 12-month chart sloped down at a 45-degree angle. At the end of the 12 months of training, his monthly turnover rate was one tenth of what it had been before the training. People stay for more than pay; people stay where they feel appreciated.

Out to Lunch

Lisa, corporate finance director for a commercial heating and air conditioning service contractor, found that paying positive attention and expressing appreciation changed her own attitude. She said,

> After being in my current role for over 20 years, I found myself lacking enthusiasm for the management part of my job. I am the type of person who needs to get my hands dirty, roll up my sleeves and do "real work." This has made it difficult for me to delegate tasks; after all, I'd rather be doing the work myself.

The installation of a new computer program pushed Lisa to make some changes. She delegated more tasks to her team during this high-demand time and found herself expressing appreciation to her team for doing work they hadn't done before. She reported,

> Over the last several weeks I've discovered a new-found purpose and enjoyment in managing people. I have come to realize that through delegation I am empowering and motivating my team. I have enjoyed setting challenging performance goals with them and then actually following up by checking in to see how they are coming along in accomplishing their goals. We are setting deadlines together. I have found that this makes for far more productive conversations in our weekly meetings.
>
> I have become five times more enthusiastic about my role as a manager! It has become natural to spontaneously hand out words of appreciation and encouragement—something that has never been easy for me. Even when one team member tried to shrug off the praise by saying "Well, isn't this is what you told me to do?"—I said, "I know I asked you to do it; I still appreciate the fact that you got it done."
>
> Last Friday, for the first time in a long time, I took my whole team out to lunch. In the past I've been too uncomfortable to do this; I was afraid conversation would be too difficult. We had a great time!

The lesson I have learned from my new engaged approach to leadership is that when I stretch beyond my comfort zone, with renewed enthusiasm and intentional focus, managing people can be a lot more fun and it brings more meaning to my work and life.

Show people that you consider them important. Let your outstanding trait be your unfailing recognition and appreciation of ability and contribution in any form. Appreciation is a powerful method for stimulating loyalty and engagement.

Home Plate: Give Insightful Praise

"Praise focusses on a quality."

Praise is the oxygen of the soul. When you give insightful praise, you nourish the essence of a person. When you praise, you are giving a lift to the spirit. Remember how fragile the human ego is. Remember how unsure you have been at times. Remember how uncertain those within your influence may be.

Praise is telling people about something you observed them doing or saying that reveals one of their personal strengths, one of their admirable qualities. The highest form of praise gives the receiver a positive reputation to live up to. They see themselves in a new light and begin to perform in harmony with this strengthened self-image. You can help grow a person with praise and appreciation, which increases their value.

Observe the Good in Others

One session of the Leadership Development Lab is titled "Observations That Empower." It's a fantastic session. After each participant makes a short presentation, other participants give them a compliment on one of the strengths they've observed. As one of our class members was struggling to give this praise, she said, "I have to think so hard."

Yes, we do have to think hard if we're going to be able to provide strengths-based praise that enlivens the receiver.

There's no lack of excellence in the performance of our customers, suppliers, coworkers, bosses, subordinates, friends, and family. The lack of excellence is often ours: our own lack of looking deeply to discover the personal qualities that drive performance.

The lesson I've learned is that if I'm going to bring out the best in others, I must be willing to think hard. If I'm going to build relationships to help others grow, I must be willing to think hard, wake up the gray matter, give praise. It's an important part of building an engaged team.

The Hire

Jodie, a human resources director, was interviewing employees for an open position in her paper mill. She told us she *focused on qualities* by using our Leadership Principles during her interviews as a basis for selection. When the interviews were over, she told each interviewee which leadership skills she had observed in them during the interview. Jodie said,

> I could see this helped make them feel good about themselves—whether or not they got the job. By telling them, at the conclusion of their interview, some of their particular strengths, they were encouraged about themselves, their potential, and their future with the paper mill.

Focus on the Positive

Most of us can spontaneously list far more negative than positive qualities. The following list may help you focus on the positive. Pick the descriptive words you want to use to praise your team members. You can add to this list as you think of additional positive, praiseworthy qualities. Remember the most powerful and effective praise points out characteristics—positive traits—about which the receiver is uncertain.

A List of Praiseworthy Qualities

Accommodating	Delightful	Gifted	Receptive
Adaptable	Determined	Good Mixer	Refined
Agreeable	Devout	Good-natured	Reflective
Ambitious	Direct	Happy	Resourceful
Attentive	Discreet	High-spirited	Responsible
Aware	Dynamic	Humble	Responsive
Big-hearted	Eager	Impressive	Sensitive
Brave	Easy-going	Innovative	Sociable
Bright	Effective	Insightful	Soft-hearted
Calm	Empathic	Inspiring	Soothing
Careful	Encouraging	Interesting	Spontaneous
Cautious	Energetic	Kind	Steady
Cheerful	Enjoyable	Knowledgeable	Stimulating
Communicative	Entertaining	Masterful	Talented
Competent	Enthusiastic	Motivating	Tenacious
Composed	Excellent	Open-minded	Thorough
Confident	Exciting	Outgoing	Thoughtful
Congenial	Expressive	Persuasive	Tolerant
Considerate	Faithful	Pleasant	Unassuming
Convincing	Fearless	Poised	Unruffled
Cooperative	Firm	Precise	Unselfish
Courageous	Flexible	Productive	Venturesome
Creative	Fluent	Punctual	Vigorous
Daring	Friendly	Quick-thinking	Willing
Decisive	Generous	Quick-witted	Wise

Choose a word a day to use in your praise, and when you have finished the list, start over again. See how it changes your outlook and the lives of others in permanent and positive ways.

> *Now a bit of praise isn't much to give,*
> *but it's dear to the hearts of all that live;*
> *and a kindly word, when the work is fair,*
> *is welcome and wanted everywhere.*
>
> Author Unknown

A Word of Caution

One important precaution is this: remember that some people, a *minority*, "puff up" under praise. Be aware of them. In most cases, the person who is "puffed up," who is arrogant and conceited, is compensating for a lack of true self-confidence. It's easy to think that praise is the last thing arrogant people need, but the opposite is true. They need reassurance. They need to develop an internal belief that they are truly valued so they can stop pretending.

Beethoven's Kiss

The pianist Andor Földes told a story that shows how praise enhances personal performance. When he was 16 and struggling with disagreements with his music teacher, he had the opportunity to play for a famous pianist, Emil von Sauer, who was the last person alive who had studied with Liszt. Földes played Bach's "Toccata in C major" and, when von Sauer requested more, Beethoven's "Pathetique" and Schumann's "Papillons." Foldes said,

> Finally, von Sauer rose and kissed me on the forehead. "My son," he said, "When I was your age I became a student of Liszt. He kissed me on the forehead after my first lesson, saying, 'Take good care of this kiss—it comes from Beethoven, who gave it to me after hearing me play.' I have waited for years to pass on this sacred heritage, but now I feel you deserve it."
>
> Nothing in my life has meant as much to me as von Sauer's praise. Beethoven's kiss miraculously lifted me out of my crisis and helped me become the pianist I am today. Soon I in turn will pass it on to the one who most deserves it.[12]

Plan to Praise

Think of someone with whom you would like to strengthen your relationship, eliminate friction, improve response, or just help grow. What positive qualities do you see? How could you express your admiration or respect for this trait? What could you say? Remember to be specific. Even though people love to be told that we appreciate them, that we value them, most people are skeptical. Praise that is not accepted is of no real value. Being specific will demonstrate that you have been paying attention, which is the prerequisite for expressing praise that will be accepted and make a positive difference.

> *"Let me be a little kinder,*
> *Let me be a little blinder*
> *To the faults of those around me.*
> *Let me praise a little more."*
> Edgar Guest

Instilling a Winning Culture

Paul, beverage manager for a wholesale food distributor, told us about an opportunity he had to shape a positive culture at his workplace:

About a month ago, right after our Turbo session on how to provide empowering coaching, I was sitting at my desk when a salesman named Mark came into my department. I overheard him telling my service tech how much he appreciated the professional job he had done in completing a recent equipment installation. He went on to say how happy his customer was with the whole job. I was embarrassed to hear how my service tech replied: "What do you want now, Mark?" Mark, a little exasperated, said, "I just came in to say thanks," turned around and walked out of the department.

About half an hour later, when I was alone with the service tech, I asked him if he was OK, if he was having any problems. His reply was "No," that everything was fine. Then I mentioned what I had observed when Mark took the time and effort to come down to our department to say thanks and give him praise for a job well done. I told him it sounded to me like he had blown him off, questioned his sincerity and honesty. I said if I were Mark, I would have a hard time telling him thanks again anytime soon.

The service tech said he understood that what he had done was wrong and thanked me for bringing it to his attention. About an hour later, I heard my technician on the phone with Mark, thanking him for the acknowledgement and apologizing for his earlier behavior.

The lesson I learned from this experience is that as soon as I see a negative behavior that mediates against teamwork, I need to respond to it, provide the needed coaching, do my part to turn things around, to create a positive team environment. If I don't do it, it won't get done.

An important part of an engaging leader's job is to be alert to unacceptable behavior and then to find *acceptable* ways to call people on it. If you don't, the culture will wind down. Cultures—groups, teams—never naturally spiral upward. Be careful when you are correcting unacceptable, demoralizing, diminishing behaviors. If *your* behavior is demeaning, diminishing, or unacceptable, you will have defeated your whole purpose.

So take a tip from Paul: wait for a private opportunity, draw attention to what has occurred, and honestly speak your own truth about how you would feel and what you would do if you were the recipient of such a comment. You may not always get as immediate a response as Paul, but you will be taking charge of your culture, your environment, and you will probably make a bigger difference than you can imagine. This is engaging leadership. It's up to you, and it requires tact and courage. Never miss an opportunity to provide culture coaching.

Distribute Evenly

Do some of your team members seem to stand out? Are others easy to overlook? Don't forget to provide acknowledgement to those who work behind the scenes, whose shine may be less obvious than the stars everyone notices. Distribute attention, approval, appreciation, and praise to every team member. You'll create a positive environment, increase engagement, and propel your team to exceed high expectations.

Actions for Engaging Leaders

- Pay positive attention for showing up.
- Give approval for being approximately right.
- Show appreciation for extra effort.
- Give insightful praise.

Benefits You Will Gain

- You'll gain the teamwork you require.
- You'll build people, helping make them successful.
- You'll improve morale.
- You'll be respected.

*"The choice of a point of view
is the initial act of a culture."*
Jose Ortega y Gasset

>>>Principle 5

See Their Point of View

Dr. Al Siebert, a practical psychologist, told us the story of his niece, who graduated with honors from the pre-med program at Lewis and Clark College. She is a brilliant young lady who studied hard and earned an outstanding G.P.A. During her senior year, her family wanted to know where she was going to medical school. At the last minute she said, "I'm not going to medical school." Instead, she decided to become a lab technician. At first it was hard for the rest of her family to see her point of view.

The prestige, power, and income associated with being an M.D. weren't nearly as important to her as having time and energy to go windsurfing in the Columbia Gorge.

When we seek to engage others, we must *see their point of view*. If they are not motivated by traditional goals and want flexible hours, like Dr. Siebert's niece, you must strive to understand what they want. How can you arrive at a win-win if you don't know what a win is for them? For some people, a raise in pay, power, or position would not be as motivating as flexible time or challenging, stimulating work. When you can anticipate people's wishes and meet those wishes before they themselves reveal them, or perhaps before they even fully realize those wishes exist, you will create engagement.

It may seem counterintuitive to first focus on someone else's point of view when you're eager to influence them and get engagement with your vision. The most natural thing to do is to let your self-interests, your own experiences, prejudices, and fears, dominate your understanding and behavior. It is difficult—in fact, it may be quite impossible—to see others' points of view in the purest sense. We are bound to our own feelings and experiences. We must pay attention, show interest, and have a desire to see the other person's point of view. The closer we come to understanding their point of view, the stronger the relationship is between us. Henry Ford said, "If there is any one secret of success, it lies in the ability to *get the other person's point of view* and see things from their angle as well as your own."

Labor, management, production, engineering, credit, and sales may have different points of view. New hires who are part of the connected generation and tenured employees with limited formal education may have different points of view. Considering all of the differences that set you apart from others—character traits, talents, needs, and interests—is an important step toward the understanding needed to successfully create an engaged team. Approach each person with their own special perspective and interests on the front of your mind.

Fast Start

Dale, controls division manager for a large construction company in eastern Washington, was considering the point of view of a new employee when he decided on a careful course of training. He told us,

> We had a new employee, an engineering technician, hired on to our crew. He had been hired to help with our efficiency and provide needed technical assistance. We were behind on developing our client O&M (operation and maintenance) manuals. I decided working on our

client's manuals would be a great way to both get the manuals up-to-date and help him start learning our unique processes.

I began his training with a review of our entire job process, starting with estimating, submitting to engineering, and finally developing client operation manuals. I went on to review with him one of our completed client operations and training manuals. This way he could see my vision of the finished product. I then had him go back over the entire process step-by-step with me.

He was a little overwhelmed but picked up pretty well on the overview of the process. I turned him loose by having him start working on a new manual for a project that is in its final phase. He stayed with it, and although it took a little longer than either of us had thought it would, the job is completed, and he seems to have a good grasp on our entire process.

The lesson I learned from this experience is when I take the proper time training new employees so they feel comfortable with their work, they will outperform usual levels of expected performance.

When you hire or promote someone, work to see their point of view. How do people feel in a new job? There is a predictable range of emotions. It doesn't matter whether you are hiring them to sweep the floor or promoting them to CEO—they are excited and scared. What do these new hires want? They want to be successful! They naturally want to know *how* to be successful. They want a clear understanding of what success looks like in their new role. They need training, reassurance, encouragement, and direction.

In fact, direction and training is encouraging. Most turnover occurs in the first 90 days. Strengthen your training and on-boarding practices and you will go a long way toward improving productivity, teamwork, and profits. This is your path to long-term productive relationships, exhilarating improvements, and success. You both win when you build the confidence of a new employee.

Changing a Charged Relationship

Marcella, HR specialist for a food distribution company in Seattle, WA, considered a difficult coworker's point of view:

> For over two months, ever since my promotion, I had been experiencing a discomforting lack of communication with one of my coworkers. She is supposed to provide me with the essential personnel information I need to successfully perform in my new position. She is the only source for this information, short of me taking several hours a week to dig it out.
>
> We have had quite a few differences of opinion about how things were handled in the past and what was the best way to execute going forward for our department's future success. I think, from her point of view, she may feel that she, instead of me, should have been promoted when the position became available. She has made it clear in subtle and not so subtle ways that she doesn't feel I am qualified for the role.
>
> After reevaluating the long term importance of this relationship, I decided to make this my "Turbo 5X Project," to "apply five times more enthusiasm" to changing my attitude toward her to improve our relationship. I focused with five times the intention and positive determination to make our working relationship fully functional. Since making that decision, to my amazement, the communication between us has been great. We talk frequently and she provides me with the answers I need to every request I have made with few questions asked.
>
> The lesson I learned is when I consider another person's point of view, it can change my outlook about a relationship, and when I decide to take responsibility

for making a relationship work, I can improve a bad, seemingly hopeless situation into a smooth-functioning, workable one.

A question I often ask is "Would you rather be right or happy?" In this case, it's possible that Marcella had every reason to say, "I'm right," but "I'm right" wasn't solving her problem, improving her relationship, or gaining the cooperation she needed. By changing her focus to making the relationship work, by taking responsibility for making it work, an amazing, almost miraculous shift occurred.

I challenge you to take a look at relationships that may not be working to your full satisfaction. Ask yourself, "If I were willing to give up being right, what might happen if I made a commitment to make this relationship work?" Why not give it a try? You don't have to try it forever. Try it for three weeks— just 21 days—and see what a difference you can make. Would you rather be right or happy?

Repeat Repair Orders

Don made a special effort to learn his team's point of view. He told us,

> Prior to becoming the regional service supervisor of the cable maintenance department at GTE, I heard about the strong feelings of resentment that some of the Beaverton crew members had about me being promoted. After learning more about why they were unhappy and resentful, I felt like much of it was based on rumor and hearsay. I realized that if we were going to succeed as a team, it would be my responsibility to take the initiative to earn their respect, trust, and confidence.
>
> I met with each crew member one-on-one, usually out in the field. My intent was to be as open and honest as possible, see their point of view, and answer their questions. I wanted to hear their goals and work expectations. Then I scheduled group meetings and

asked for collective ideas and input on what was needed for me to do the best job possible.

By showing a genuine concern for the crews' feelings and demonstrating respect for their points of view, they were able to voice what were important issues to them. One of the key crew leaders told me that the crew's fears about me were gone, and that I could count on his and the rest of the crews' full support. I fully expect my relationship with the cable maintenance crew to be based on understanding, respect, and trust.

The rest of the story: during the months following Don's promotion, his team had the lowest number of repeat repair orders ever in the decades-long history of his department's district. His crew members' attention to detail is key evidence of their high level of engagement.

Keep Your Cool

Jerry, service manager for a commercial heating and air conditioning service contractor, considered his customer's point of view:

Last Thursday morning, my technician, Scott, called me from one of our customer's sites. He said there was a bad compressor in one of the water source heat pumps he was performing routine preventative maintenance on. This is not good news for our customer, and none of us enjoy being the bearer of bad tidings. I asked my operations supervisor to put a price together for the replacement pump. Including installation, it came to $2,600.00.

When Scott gave the price to Dan, our customer, he started yelling at Scott about how much money it was: "Why are you ripping me off? I am going to have to call for prices from other contractors from now on," and he continued to rant.

Scott quietly waited for Dan to calm down a little, then in a professional tone said, "How about if I ask Jerry to call you directly about the work authorization. I'm sure you guys can work this out."

Dan felt comfortable that Scott came up with a workable next step solution, so I called Dan and told him I had figured on eight hours to change his compressor. "Scott says he can do it in six, so let's do this job for time and materials. I guarantee you it will be less than the $2,600.00 for the repair." Scott did the job in 4½ hours and we saved Dan $600.00.

The lesson I learned from this experience is that successful problem solving can be a multi-step team process, and using the principle "See Their Point of View" is wise when things heat up and you are on the receiving end of a complaint.

A line in the song "How Can I Keep from Singing" says, "No storm can shake my inmost calm." What if you and I could find a place inside ourselves that was so calm and so connected, where there was no storm, no circumstance, accusatory customer complaints included, that could shake our inmost calm?

Today, as you're doing all the many things you must do, take a moment and notice that there is a place inside of you that is independent of anything that's going on the outside. Nurture that place. Living from this place of peace will make you a truly powerful person. You will s*ee their point of view* with no need to be right.

> *"When we are no longer able to change a situation,*
> *we are challenged to change ourselves."*
> Victor Frankl

Actions for Engaging Leaders

- Put positive energy into improving any not so great relationship in your world.
- When you are on the receiving end of a client's complaint, see their point of view.
- Give new employees the training they need to feel competent.

Benefits You Will Gain

- You'll experience less stress at work and in your personal life.
- You will be able to effectively communicate with everyone on your team.
- You'll experience stress-free problem solving and a happy customer.
- You'll have employees who perform beyond your expectations.

*"It is the disease of not listening
that I am troubled with."*
William Shakespeare

>>>Principle 6

Be an Active Listener

At the close of a ten-hour Leadership Training Advance session, I was beat—I mean really worn out. I fell asleep at 9:00 p.m. and slept right through until the alarm went off at 6:30 the next morning. The way I conducted this program should have been pretty easy on me. Participants are the center of attention; they do 80 percent of the talking.

The next morning, when I talked with the president of the company, who had been actively involved the previous day, he said, "I wasn't tired. It didn't feel like a ten-hour day to me; it felt more like a three- or four-hour day. I was stimulated and invigorated."

"Why was I so tired?" I asked my wife, who had helped me by doing the camera work.

She said, "Because you listened to every word spoken, and listening is work."

Of course, she was right. I did listen to every word, and listening is work. For most of us, listening—setting aside our own agenda and really listening—takes more effort than rambling on.

Be an Active Listener!

The action required to understand another person's point of view is to listen actively. Engaging leaders encourage the other person to do a great deal of the talking. They ask questions to learn the attitudes and ideas that might otherwise go unspoken. Never interrupt, step on their lines, or top their story. If you do, the other person may clam up even though they still have plenty left to say. One of the most difficult things for most of us to do is fully listen, especially when we don't agree.

Listening pays off. Remember, most people don't listen. Since good listeners are in short supply and in high demand, they are prized and appreciated.

Rotary Club

Before I spoke for the Eastside Rotary Club, club members introduced guests at their tables. The club member who introduced Bob Munger, our associate, said, "I only met this gentleman a few moments ago—I don't know him that well. The one thing I can tell you is he is a good listener."

I was so proud of Bob and the way his professionalism reflected on Turbo Leadership Systems. What a great qualification—to be introduced as a good listener. I'd like to have it said of me that I'm a "good listener." One of the most important parts of engaging leadership is being a good listener. Good listeners make our best friends. Good listeners are the best salesmen. Good listeners are the best spouses. Good listeners are the best parents. Good listeners are the best. So, let's turn up our listening.

Call Back

My associate Steve and I arrived at our 11:30 a.m. appointment with a prospective client in downtown Portland. We had met with this client a week before, but we were back again. Why? Not to try and sell anything, and certainly not for an idle visit. We were back to be sure we had really listened, to be sure we understood the prospective client's desires, needs, and objectives. We had outlined our understanding in our "talking paper" with several questions for clarification. Again, we listened. As it turned out, we were right on with our understanding. There were a couple of points of clarification. We walked out with more confidence, enthusiasm, and conviction about the important difference we could make.

The easiest way to influence people and impress them favorably is to encourage them to talk about their interests, opinions, and problems. Encourage them to talk by asking questions. Be certain that the questions you ask display respect for the other person's knowledge. Make it a definite part of your approach to listen attentively when others are speaking. Simple enough, isn't it? Yet how many people have we encountered who are so eager to tell their story that we cannot get a word in edgewise? When you listen to others on your team and acknowledge the validity of their beliefs, you have taken a major step that will encourage them to engage, whether they agree with you wholeheartedly or not. It's more likely people will consider your way of thinking when you have acknowledged their way of thinking by listening.

Here are some questions you might use (in neutral tones) to open the other person up as you listen actively:

- What do you like best about your job?
- What is the most difficult part of your job?
- How long have you been in this role?
- What did you do before?
- When and where did it happen?
- Who was involved? Anyone else?
- What did they say?
- What happened then?
- Tell me more.
- Why do you think that happened?
- How do you see that working?

- Why do you feel that way?
- What will you do differently next time?
- Where would you use/put it?
- Where do you want to start?

Listen, really listen to every answer. You may be pleasantly surprised at how much you can learn.

Customer Council

I recently visited the manufacturer of quality household hardware who has been in business over 40 years. Displayed in the lobby are photos of all their employees with the tenure of each employee prominently displayed. It was obvious that they've had little turnover. As the plant manager and I were first getting acquainted, I complimented him on his lack of turnover. He said, "Oh, there are about 16 people whose pictures we haven't put up yet. We are adding to our team."

As we toured the plant he proudly pointed out the old and new product lines, all of the production systems and equipment—from casting to packaging—and the final gleaming products.

I said, "Tell me more about your new products."

He told me, "We formed a dealer advisory council this past year and had our first meeting last summer. The dealers on the council gave us some great product ideas that we've implemented, and our new products have created a measurable increase in sales. Members of our customer council can walk into our plant any time and talk to anyone on the floor, from the people who do the castings to those who do the painting, polishing, and packaging."

Wow, I thought, what a great example of empowerment and listening to the customer, of being customer-driven, and of the benefits that can be gained when you really listen and act on the advice given. Sales for this company have gone up because the company listened to its customers. Their labor costs have gone down because they have engaged people on the floor and eliminated unnecessary layers of management.

Engaging leaders find ways to ask and listen to their customers, both their internal and external customers.

Allergic to Self-Centered Conversations

Before speaking at a luncheon meeting, I was seated between two people. The person on my right said something about being allergic to wheat. The other said, "Oh, really? I have daughters who are allergic to wheat," and on and on they went, non-stop, for what felt like 30 minutes. I'm sure it wasn't more than ten, but the topic wasn't of interest to me, so it seemed long. These two were caught up in their own world. How easy it is for us to get caught up in our own web of drama. When we do, we are boring.

If you like to be an engaging leader, don't dominate conversations with your travels, your interests, your allergies, your illnesses, where you've been, what you're going to do, and how you feel about things. Instead, ask others, "What are your plans?" "Where will you be going?" "Have you been there before?" "What were your experiences that made you decide to go back?" You will help others open up, and your ability to stimulate conversation and bring the best out in others will be noticed.

All Wet

Trevor, service manager for a commercial HVAC contractor, discovered that not listening can be costly. He told us,

> I had just started in my new position as Installation Supervisor for a residential HVAC company. We were working on a new residential construction job, a 45-home subdivision. As supervisor of the installation crew, one of my responsibilities was to make sure all the supply air ducts were properly installed.

From time to time new homeowners would stop by to see how their homes were progressing, so I gave them a tour of the house. One of the best features of these new homes was a large bay offset in the formal living room. As we entered the room, I noticed that there wasn't a supply register in the bay offset. Josh, one of my lead installers, was walking by, so I asked him to cut a hole in a certain spot that I picked out. Josh really didn't care for my authority at the time, and with a big smile on his face, he proceeded to cut the hole right where I had told him to. He wasn't even halfway through his cut when we had "old faithful" rushing into the new house.

Josh had come to me earlier that morning with some concerns, but I thought I knew everything I needed to know and brushed him off. After everything was under control, Josh looked at me and said, "I tried to tell you this morning that the main water line had been moved!"

The lesson I learned from this experience is to take the time to listen, especially when I'm sure of myself and think I know everything.

Ask yourself honestly: are there times when you are acting like Trevor? Are there any times when associates are subtly sabotaging your projects? Pledge today to actively listen to everyone on your team. Instead of wanting to sabotage your work, they'll see themselves as valued members of your team, engaged in meeting team objectives successfully.

In from the Cold

Tom, operations supervisor for a hardwood lumber plant in northern Pennsylvania, told us about a time his manager didn't listen:

It was on a cold winter day at around 9:00 in the morning. I had been working for approximately three hours out of doors in ten-degree weather with a wind chill of zero or below. I was trying to keep rows of inbound logs scaled and marked, to keep two log lifts busy so our saw mill would not be held up for a lack of log supply. I had worked through my scheduled break and just a little bit longer to finish another row for pick up. Then I walked into the boiler house break room and sat down to have a hot cup of coffee and a sandwich, and to thaw out a little bit.

I had just taken my first bite when the production manager, Jack, walked into the break room. He looked at me and, without asking why I was there, proceeded to chew me out. He didn't accept my reply that I had worked through my regular break time to keep things going for the saw mill and had just come in for a quick break. He told me to take my break at the scheduled time or not at all. He went on to say, "If you don't like it, 5,000 Cuban refugees who have their applications in at the office can easily replace you."

Talk about belittling and diminishing! If I had expected any acknowledgement, appreciation, or gratitude for going the extra mile—for extending myself into the job for the betterment of the company and my team—I had another thing coming. I finished my sandwich and coffee and went back to work. Nothing really changed except my attitude toward Jack and, of course, the company and management who put him in the position of power and control he so enjoyed.

The lesson I learned from that experience is to get the facts before I go off halfcocked. I learned the importance of listening to what my crew has to tell me before I reach any conclusion.

Silent Fix

Jim, a pipefitter foreman for a Northwest mechanical contracting company, took active listening home:

In the past, when my wife had a problem, I would jump in like the hero I want to be and try to "fix" everything. This seldom worked and usually frustrated both of us.

Since learning about being an "active listener," I have applied this principle with my wife. Just last week she told me about something that was troubling her. She explained in great detail what had happened and her feelings about it. I sat quietly, listening intently, showing that I really did want to understand.

When she finished, I remained quiet. I'm not sure how it felt to her; it sure felt awkward to me. Truth be told, I was biting my tongue. After a few moments of silence, my wife asked me for my opinion and what I would do. That was quite a shift! We discussed the situation and some possible solutions. I didn't try to fix it; I just offered her encouraging support.

The lesson I learned from this experience is the importance of listening, caring, and showing my support. I have found myself practicing this with my crew. They have feelings too, and sometimes they just need to vent.

Listening—active listening—is one of the best ways to acknowledge and support the important people in our lives. When you listen, you say, "Your story is important to me. What you have to say matters. You matter."

The next time someone is trying to sort out what to do next, why not say to yourself, "The fix is in silence." If you must speak, why not start this way: "Well, what do you think?"

Listening, really listening to the other person is one of the most respectful, acknowledging things we can do. "The average person talks too much, especially if they have a good command of language," said Elbert Gary about negotiating an agreement. "A wise leader keeps a close mouth."[13] Great leaders have learned to make a fine art of listening. They know listening is more than mere silence, more than waiting for their turn to talk. They take a genuine interest in what others are saying; even more, they take the trouble to display their interest by actively listening. They mirror the behaviors, posture, and stance of the other person. They paraphrase and summarize what they have heard, and give the other person the opportunity to clarify what they've said and, if needed, to explain further.

Techniques to Improve Your Listening

1. Shut up—close your mouth. You can't talk and listen at the same time.

2. Recognize that listening is something you do for personal success. You don't listen just to be nice to others. Listening earns power, respect, love, and helps you gain the information you need to be effective.

3. Want to listen better. View listening as a small investment of time and energy that produces an enormous return in understanding.

4. Become less self-centered. You're about the only one who believes that you and what you have to say is more important than the other person and what they have to say. Maybe you're wrong.

5. Prepare to listen. When possible, think about the speaker and the topic in advance. Set goals for what you hope to learn.

6. Work at listening. People speak at an average rate of 120 words per minute. The average listening capacity is about 480 words per minute, or four times faster. This differential results in our minds wandering when another person is speaking. If you can give the speaker a little more concentration—say about 200 wpm of your listening capacity—your mind won't wander. You achieve this by making eye contact, by thinking intently about what is being said, by standing or sitting upright, and by asking questions.

7. Check for nonverbal cues. Look for what the speaker may be telling you through body language. Listen for tone of voice.

8. Hold your fire. Refrain from giving any impression that you disagree while the person is talking. Pretend that everything they are saying is valid (it is, in the sense that they believe it) at least until they stop talking.

9. Don't plan your response while the other person is talking. You only need a few seconds to think about your response before giving it. The other person will wait for you. There's nothing wrong with a little silence between that person's words and your response. Trust yourself. You will know what to say.

10. Overcome distractions. Ignore noisy surroundings. Fight distractions in the situation or in the speaker. Instead, let their little idiosyncrasies be the stimulus to listen with greater interest.

11. Prioritize understanding. Say to yourself, "Right now, understanding this person's ideas, thinking and feelings is the most important thing in my life." This is the time to focus all of your listening capacity on the speaker. You'll know you've done your job if you are exhausted afterward.

12. Defer judgment. Suspend judgments while the person is talking. Practice making the decisions you need to make about people and events without coming to final conclusions. When you decide what is true or right, you spend your energy defending your conclusions, and you're not likely to listen to disagreement with it.

> *"One of the reasons that we find so few persons rational and agreeable in conversation is that there is hardly a person who does not think more of what he wants to say than of his answer to what is said."*
> Francois De La Rochefoucauld

Actions for Engaging Leaders

- Listen for the facts before you make a judgment.
- Be aware of the other person's need to be heard.
- Be an active listener; don't interrupt with your answers, opinions, and judgments.

Benefits You Will Gain

- Others will respect you.
- You will create a dedicated, engaged team.
- Trust will increase.

"Great leaders are not the ones in the spotlight, they're the ones leading the applause."
Author Unknown

>>>Principle 7

Play Yourself Down

Over 40 years ago, I walked into the office of the national sales manager for Eli Lilly, one of the most successful pharmaceutical firms in America. Frank greeted me warmly, and we talked about the sales training that I was teaching at the time in downtown Detroit. I noticed the sign on his desk: "There's no limit to what you can accomplish if you don't care who gets the credit."

Frank enrolled in my sales class, was a great participant, and subsequently sent many of his salespeople through the program. As I reflect on the experience now, I realize the credit Frank gave me at the time for the improved performance of his salespeople was just one example of the many ways he employed the principle of playing himself down.

An integral part of engaging leadership and improving communication is playing yourself down. That pithy bit of advice I saw for the first time in Frank's office, and have seen and thought about many times since, is true: "There is no limit to what you can accomplish if you do not care who gets the credit."

The engaging leader has learned to set aside ego's desire to be the star of the show. They know that securing engaged commitment requires they first be willing to do what is best for the team, to think beyond self-interest, and it is only in this willingness to sacrifice their own ego that they can expect to lead others with integrity to make sacrifices for the good of a cause, to put forth discretionary effort for the good of the team.

There is a subtle paradox in a style of leadership which admits fallibility. Strong, competent leaders who willingly play themselves down are the leaders others eagerly raise up. Engaging leaders encourage others to be out in front in the limelight while they keep themselves in the background whenever possible. Consider the opposite kind—leaders who must continually bolster their own egos by managing things so that the credit goes to themselves, fearful of relinquishing control and delegating authority to others. Their teams are likely to relish those leaders' downfall instead of respecting their leadership.

All Dressed Up and Going Nowhere

During a discussion of management after our Cultural Benchmark employee opinion meeting, someone shared a story about the owner of the company where he formerly worked, who apparently lived by the maxim "It's all about *me*":

> The owner walked in during a short lull in the phones ringing. It had been an extremely busy day and we had been hustling for hours. He didn't ask how the day had been going or check our sales tickets for the day. He just saw us without customers on the phone and said, "What are you guys doing? See these shoes? $500! See these pants? $300! See this shirt? $200! I can't dress like this unless you guys stay on those phones!"

It's obvious this manager was focused on his own desires instead of engaging his team. He managed by observation, jumped to conclusions, and alienated his team with his egocentric rant. Sometimes egocentrism is easier to recognize in others than in ourselves. It takes humility to examine ourselves, to willingly consider how others see us, how they experience their interactions with us. The insight you gain from humbly considering how others experience your presence, your interactions with them, is an important step toward being an engaging leader.

The challenge of many managers is appearing egotistical, like they know it all. You'll never engage others successfully with that reputation. Authority gives you power. The need for bragging should be replaced with finding a way to play yourself down. Anyone who wishes to maximize their personal potential, to make the most of their opportunities as a leader, is interested in healthy self-assessment and gaining an awareness of how they are perceived by others. The gap that exists between accurate self-assessment and the reality of how others see us is often quite wide. You'll never get a window into the "blind self" without the willingness to play yourself down; this takes true humility.

Make it clear that you consider the results of the project at hand far more important than who gets credit for its achievement. When leading your team, be careful to put the organization's mission, purpose, and performance standards ahead of what you want. The personal pronoun *I* is minimized and instead of *I*, the wise engaging leader refers to what *we* are doing, why *we* exist, the difference *we* make. The authority, the genesis of power, isn't the leader's personal force. Instead, the "boss" is the organization's mission and purpose. The engaging leader asks team members to align with *our* values, not what *I* demand, what *I* want—instead, what *we* stand for.

Give your team full credit for successes. Avoid pretension of any kind. A self-deprecating comment or a story about the time you blew it is often an effective means of gaining respect and engaged effort. This is how you can stamp out fear of trying something new, of taking the initiative. This is how you emphasize your commitment to excellence and draw the contrast between obtainable excellence and impossible perfection. With your willingness to play yourself down, you make it clear you are not perfect, you do not expect perfection—you expect excellence.

Award Winner

Eric Hoffman, project manager for the renovation of the Multnomah County Central Library in downtown Portland, OR, helped everyone feel like an important team member. The library building, which was designed by A.E. Doyle, was originally built in 1913 for a cost of $465,000. The renovation contract was approximately $17 million. Eric told us,

> The challenge was to upgrade the building to modern standards while restoring the interior to match its original appearance and ensure its historic merit. The major modernization elements included seismic reinforcing to improve building safety and meet present-day code, completely new HVAC systems to meet modern comfort standards and preserve the library's contents, and completely new electrical systems, including computer networking capabilities throughout the facility. We gutted the entire interior of the building in order to install all of the new elements.

> Throughout the process, we worked with historical experts, along with numerous extraordinary subcontractors, who brought forward the craftsmanship necessary to meet all of the demanding project goals. There were many old European journeymen craftsmen and apprentice craftsmen who were knowledgeable about the fine arts of plaster, terrazzo, stone, and woodwork.

> At our weekly progress meetings, I always made a point of introducing any new experts into the team as the project unfolded. I told about their background, recent successes, and the important part they were playing in the success of the project.

> It was a thrilling experience from start to finish.

In recognition of the project's success, the team received the Project of the Year Award for Historical Preservation from the National American Public Works Association.

The lesson I learned from this experience is that outstanding results can be achieved when the individual craftsmen are recognized and fully involved, when they are made to feel like members of an elite team.

The most important part of this brief story is the simple idea of honoring each member of the team for the important part they play. The way Eric chose to play himself down was by honoring each member of the team for the important part they played, introducing them respectfully as important team members, even if their part of the job was relatively small. This created a spirit of cooperation and high morale.

Eric's introductions made clear that each person's part was extremely important for the overall project to be successful. In some cases, their part may have only been veneer. There could have been an inclination to downplay their importance, since the original intention was to make the building more structurally sound. In other cases, their part may have been hidden—perhaps an internal structural element that was subsequently covered up by fancy woodwork. Including everyone, honoring them and their role in the upgrade and restoration, as Eric said, was vital to the success of the project.

How does this relate to you and your business? Chances are you have important suppliers without whom you cannot be successful, maybe some part-time employees or even the infamous "temps" who are often dropped into work assignments with almost no orientation. Too often, these temps are treated as "hands" rather than as important members of the team. If you'd like to improve the performance and the outcome of your team, honor every member of the organization as if their contribution is vitally important—for, in fact, it is.

To inspire enthusiasm and loyalty in associates, share the limelight for successes. Be ready to help shoulder the blame for mistakes.

"The greater thou art, the more humble thyself."
The Apocrypha

Letting Go of the Seat

Delegating responsibilities is an important part of being a leader. It can be hard. Our egos and our fears can get in the way.

When I taught one of my sons to ride a bike, I held onto the back of the seat and ran alongside him as he learned. At what I thought was the right moment, I let go. He kept going, a little shaky, a little wobbly. When he tried to look back to see if I was watching, he fell, getting a bit scraped up. After a little bit of first aid, he wanted to try again. Eventually, he could ride with no trouble at all.

Delegating tasks is a bit like letting go of the bike seat. What if I had insisted on holding onto the seat every time my son had wanted to ride? I had to risk letting him crash so that he could really go places, and go faster than I could run! If you haven't given a person enough room to fail, you haven't fully delegated. They are not fully empowered. If you think you're the only one who can do it right, that your way is the only right way, you'll fail to properly delegate. Instead of an engaged team, focused on the goals of the company or organization, you'll have a bunch of individuals focused on salvaging some of their self-respect.

Goals Exceeded

At the 90-day follow-up accountability session of Turbo's Leadership Team Advance for the top nine managers of a major mass merchandiser, the director of operations came up to me and said, "I want to tell you how we were able to get a 20-plus percent increase in sales last month."

"I want to know!" I said.

"Well, at the close of the last day of the month, we still had a few hundred thousand dollars to go to hit our goal. One of our store managers called around to each of our stores to ask them what their sales were for the day. Then she told the other managers that she was going to stay open an extra 30 minutes. Most of the stores joined her. We sold the additional $300,000 to reach our goal."

The chairman of the company then chimed in: "The thing I'm most proud of is that our store managers felt they had the necessary authority. They were sufficiently empowered to make the decision to stay open without having to check with the operations manager or the president of the company, without having a board meeting."

Delegation means that whoever is assigned responsibility for implementing a project truly has the authority to make decisions required for success. Sometimes this requires winning the cooperation of other departments or personnel who are used to the status quo. Hold them accountable to work with the person now in charge instead of coming back to you.

Give those you delegate all the authority they need, including authority over personnel. If you give someone the task of turning around a failing department but tell her she can't discipline or discharge the owner's nephew, you haven't properly delegated. If you don't trust them with personnel decisions, it's not fair to put them in that job—you can't hold them accountable for results.

When you are delegating well, the person to whom you've delegated a task or project is clear on the intended outcome and parameters that influence their performance. They know you will never second-guess their decisions, actions, and style as long as they are achieving agreed-upon goals.

Sabotage

Ernie, shop foreman for a metals fabrication company, told us how he and his associate, Walt, had been friends for over 20 years, yet in the past few years, the relationship had deteriorated badly. He explained,

> When I would assign him a fabrication project, I would purposely give very few instructions, and, of course, I didn't give him the context of the job. I didn't give him the big picture, didn't give him the "why" because I felt he always did it his way anyway. Then I would condemn him behind his back for not doing it the way I wanted it done. He would complain to others that my instructions were vague and that he never knew what was expected of him, saying, "I guess I'm supposed to be a mind reader."
>
> I decided that now was the time to get our relationship back to where it had been four or five years ago. I started out by complimenting Walt on the jobs he had completed in the last two or three weeks. When he was starting a new job for me, I went out of my way to explain what I had in mind when I estimated the job. I told him the big picture, the number of labor hours we had bid, how the customer planned to use the piece, and where it fit into the customer's overall project.
>
> The next day Walt came into my office with some additional questions. After answering his questions, I asked him for his ideas on how he would build the piece if he were going to install it. When he finished telling me, I said, "Great idea. Go ahead and do it that way!" I didn't let on that I had already thought of doing it the way he explained. I didn't steal his pride or deflate him by devaluing his contribution.

The lesson I learned from this experience is the importance of being more explicit in all of my instructions, and the power of listening to validate the other person's ideas. I learned when I am a little more understanding, people respond favorably. Jobs get done the right way the first time, and my team takes more pride in their work.

Take the responsibility for being understood. If people don't understand you, perhaps you haven't communicated clearly enough in your delegating. Remember: it is your job as an engaging leader to be understood. You don't need to be the one who has all the ideas or all the answers. Don't be afraid to say, "I could be wrong; I frequently am!" Always ask for input from those who are closest to the work.

Trainee

Debra had a new employee who was making mistakes and wouldn't ask for help. Initially, Debra was focusing only on the mistakes. She adopted a new strategy and began to focus on praising the new employee. She also played herself down by telling about the times she made mistakes when she was learning the job. The new secretary is now working harder and is not afraid to say, "I need help."

Sharing your own mistakes can help employees see you as a fellow human being and give them the courage to try new tasks without the fear of blowing it.

To establish a good reputation and gain the respect of others, keep in mind that modesty and sound self-promotion go hand in hand. Take special care to be modest about those things you have done, or those qualities you possess which are already recognized, or which are bound to be noticed. Remember that the credit which others give you on their own accord is always greater than any credit which you may gain by claiming it yourself. Be modest and establish a reputation for modesty.

Don't downplay yourself completely. If some of your worthwhile achievements are fairly certain to be overlooked altogether, see to it that they come to the attention of the right people at the right time. This can be done without fanfair. In fact, a self-generated report that shows achievement, trends in progress, and breakthroughs in performance can go a long way toward proving progress, even dramatizing successes, without your claiming credit. If your organization isn't good at seeing, measuring, and celebrating progress, you will add great value by initiating the practice of measuring your own progress and reporting it.

> *"Do not confuse humility with humiliation."*
> Alan Cohen

Independent Thinker

A young executive friend of ours is extremely capable but also an independent thinker, and, occasionally, a bit impatient. We asked him if this had caused him any problems in his company, where he seems to be making excellent progress.

"Not really," he said. "Fortunately, my boss is very understanding."

Recently this young man went to see his boss to ask to be relieved of membership on a policy committee where his views often disagreed with those of more senior members. "I'm sorry," he told his boss, "but when I disagree with something strongly, it goes against my nature to sit by and say nothing, or act as if I approve. Life might be a lot easier for everyone if I weren't on the committee."

"I'd prefer that you stay on the committee, Bill," said his boss. "You think clearly and express yourself well. I'm always interested in what you think, especially when you disagree with me. When you disagree, you help us see and consider the other side of the picture. That's a big help. Don't underestimate its importance to me and to the company."

Bill's boss could have jumped at the chance to fill Bill's spot on the committee with someone more compliant, but he played himself down and appreciated Bill's contributions, even though they often disagreed.

If you have two managers in your company who always agree about everything, you may have one too many managers.

Surrounded by Strength

In discussing the reason why people fail or succeed, Edward Decker, then president of the National Bank of Minneapolis, shared an astute observation:

> One of the things I like to see . . . is a person at the head of a business with a lot of strong people around them. If a leader will not select strong assistants, possibly for fear they may displace [the leader] or not do as they're told, the leader is not a big enough person to be at the head of the organization. Strong leaders will not always do just as they are told, to be sure. But it is not easy to run a business today with a convention of parrots. In a vigorous, growing organization, a great many important decisions are to be left to people in subordinate positions. You can't have a healthy big business any other way.[14]

Be ready to sacrifice your vanity when you choose and interact with your associates and friends. Find associates more successful than yourself. Seek friends whom you can admire and look up to. To create the engaged effort and innovation required for continuous improvement, don't surround yourself with "a convention of parrots."

Actions for Engaging Leaders

- Share your own mistakes from time to time.
- Share the limelight for successes with your team.

- When you delegate tasks, give those you delegate all the authority they need.

Benefits You Will Gain

- You'll inspire enthusiasm and loyalty in your team.
- Those you delegate to will be able to accomplish the team's goals.
- Your team will possess the courage needed on the road of continuous improvement.

"If you go through life convinced that your way is always best, all the new ideas in the world will pass you by."

Akio Morita

>>>Principle 8

Validate Their Ideas

Phil, project manager of an industrial commercial paint contractor, needed to engage his crews for their own safety. Some of their new projects called for the application of highly toxic Xylene-based paint products, which required the crew to wear new high-test respirators. Phil told us,

> I went into action, and after what I thought was a thorough search looking around on my own, I bought new, improved respirators that I thought would meet all our requirements. The new respirators were perfect technically—no fumes got through—but unfortunately the crew didn't like them and wouldn't wear them because they were very uncomfortable. So from a practical point of view, they didn't meet our needs at all.
>
> After spending $500 on respirators that I thought would solve our problem, I was no closer to a solution than when I started. I finally decided to ask our crew, the people who actually wear the respirators on a daily basis, for their input. We talked about all the different types of respirators that are available. We discussed their strengths and potential weaknesses. After a thorough discussion, getting everyone's ideas, points of view and

input, we agreed on a respirator everyone was happy with.

The lesson I learned from this experience is that those who are closest to the work, involved in the actual use of the equipment, are the ones who should be included in the decision about what equipment we buy. It just makes sense, and it demonstrates the importance of validating their ideas.

In the surveys we've conducted of more than 10,000 employees, fewer than 50 percent say "I am included in important decisions that affect my work." There is ample evidence that these employees are not fully engaged. Validating your team's ideas is an excellent way to secure their engagement.

Assistant's Assistance

Eileen, vice president of human resources for a dental equipment manufacturer, found a solution to a problem by asking her assistant for ideas:

I was in the process of identifying employees who would be excellent candidates to become corporate trainers for our world-class manufacturing program. I had found all but one candidate. I was running out of time and didn't know where else to look. When I told my assistant about my dilemma and asked for her input, she suggested one of our warehouse employees. She described his excellent speaking abilities, which she had noticed during an on-site interpersonal communication course she had taken with him.

I interviewed him and asked him if he would be interested in the opportunity for growth and added contribution. He was really excited, and during our week-long certification training process, turned out to be a talented, energetic, and enthusiastic trainer. He's one of our best "crowd pleasers."

I continue to validate my assistant's ideas by asking for her input, and she feels free to give it. The lesson I learned is if I seek the input of others, I find answers to problems in places I would not have thought to look.

Square Dancing

One way to validate others' ideas is to ask for and then listen to them. Bob was given the responsibility of planning the annual Western Square Dance Jubilee for his square-dancing club. The last Jubilee had been a flop. Bob wanted next year's planning session to be positive, not a finger-pointing session, so he did something that had never been done before. He set up an easel in the conference room and asked everyone for ideas to make next year's Jubilee more successful. As they spoke, he wrote down the various responsibilities and everything that would be required to make next year's Jubilee a success. He asked each committee member to develop a checklist for their responsibility.

Bob didn't know how people would react to the idea of checklists and accountability in a volunteer group. To his surprise, they gave him all of their detailed job descriptions and complete checklists of what they needed to do by the end of the meeting. By letting it be their idea, he gained their full engagement and initiated a high level of teamwork.

Railroaded

While Vim was on vacation, he was elected (or should I say, railroaded?) into the presidency of his Scandinavian Club. Partly because most of the club members were older than him, Vim found it difficult to implement any new ideas. No matter what he suggested, it seemed to get shot down. Then Vim tried a new strategy. He asked the group for their ideas on how to increase membership, have more interesting programs, attract a bigger turnout, and provide the services the club was originally designed to provide. Astoundingly, they had great ideas, many of which were the very ideas Vim had been hoping to see someone implement. Vim told us "They not only thought they were great ideas, they've been acting on these new ideas. Our club has more and happier members now than we've had for many years."

Whenever possible, engaging leaders let plans bubble up from the team and validate their team's ideas by acting on them. Surround yourself with good people and then validate their ideas. You will create hearty engagement.

Brainstorming

You can introduce brainstorming as a way to generate ideas to reduce costs, increase sales, and improve safety and quality. Here's how Brad used brainstorming to validate the ideas of his team and improve performance:

> We have eight trucks and it seemed like we were not using them to their full potential—too much overtime, late deliveries, and drivers with poor attitudes. I decided to buy a flip chart and have a green-light brainstorming session with our drivers. I explained the problem and said that for two minutes I wanted them to suggest any ideas they might have on how to better utilize our trucks.
>
> In just two minutes we generated fifteen ideas, three of which we could put into use immediately. These solutions were very simple and will probably save at least ten hours per week per branch. The best part was that when I asked for their help, I got it, and everyone left the meeting with a renewed sense of commitment to their jobs.
>
> The lesson I learned is when I have a problem, I can use brainstorming to get everyone involved in finding a practical solution that everyone supports.

B. Y. 0. S. S.

I asked members of our Turbo team to come into my office. I wanted to develop a flyer we could mail to our friends inviting them to an end-of-the-summer yard and pool party. "First, let's decide when." Someone left the room and brought in our planning calendar. "Now, what will we say to get attention?" Someone said, "Back to the future." "How about flashback?" "How about flashback splash?" "Great! Flashback splash." "Great! Let's make it B.Y.O.S.S." "What's B.Y.O.S.S.?" "Bring Your Own Success Story." "Fabulous!" And on it went.

In less than 20 minutes, we developed a far better flyer than I or any one of us working alone would probably have developed in days. What I learned from this experience is the power of synergism—the whole is greater than the sum of the parts. With synergism, two plus two equals eight or 64 or some multiplier that's off the scale. Creative, positive, directed brainstorming as a team resulted in better ideas than any one person could possibly generate. I was reminded of the feeling of self-worth, belonging, contribution, and value—all aspects of validation—that I gained from participating with others in this meaningful creative effort.

Stop for a moment. Get your customers or coworkers together and have a brief brainstorming session: a directed, creative thinking session. You'll create synergistic power that will help you solve problems quickly with relative ease. More importantly, the fact that you are listening will validate your team and increase their engagement.

Idea Blockade

Dr. J. P. Guilford, one of the founders of the psychology of creativity, said that creativity—the quality needed to become an innovator—can be deliberately developed.[15] One way is to remove the "mental blocks" that stand in the way of ideas. I believe the most important mental blocks are these:

1. Unawareness of the fact that each of us is gifted with creative potential.

2. Failure to realize that all of us can do much to make ourselves more creative.

3. Unwillingness to try, and to keep trying, to think up new and better ideas.

The biggest mental blocks are those movies in the mind that play on our fear of rejection or failure. One antidote to fear is the energy generated by brainstorming.

How to Brainstorm

All of the research on creativity and problem solving has supported the idea that the process of brainstorming leads to greater creativity, better solutions to problems, and engaged commitment to solutions. When you have a complex problem to solve or a new campaign to design, gather several minds and brainstorm your way to innovative, creative success!

Getting a group of people with diverse ideas and perceptions to brainstorm effectively takes more than simply plopping them down into chairs in the same room and expecting a miracle. Productive brainstorming takes organization. Because the creativity inside each person is best unleashed in a relaxed atmosphere, you might want to throw a brainstorming "party" to put people in a positive frame of mind right from the start.

Brainstorming is a process in which people generate as many ideas as possible *without evaluation*. This is key. Evaluating the ideas happens after as many ideas as possible are generated. Brainstorming can be done in several ways:

Freewheeling: In "freewheeling," the preferred way to brainstorm, you let ideas flow. Everyone contributes ideas spontaneously. This method encourages creativity as people build on each other's ideas. The disadvantage is that quieter members of the group may not speak up, and you may miss some valuable ideas.

Taking Turns: In a "taking turns" process, people present their ideas one at a time in sequence. The advantage is that everyone gets equal time to speak up and quieter people are more likely to contribute. The disadvantage is that it stifles spontaneity and sometimes members forget their ideas by the time their turn arrives. With this method, members should be allowed to "pass" if they have no suggestions.

Paper Pass: With this approach, everyone puts ideas on a slip of paper and passes them in to the facilitator. The advantage is that some people may be more candid and creative with their anonymity preserved. The disadvantage is not being able to hear other members' ideas, which often trigger add-on creativity.

It is best to choose the style most comfortable for your team or do some combination of the three methods, perhaps starting with "Taking Turns" or "Paper Pass" and then opening the floor to "Freewheeling."

Getting Caught Up

Rick, a machine shop supervisor for an equipment manufacturer, told us,

I decided to hold a brainstorming session with the members of my business unit. The subject was "How can we eliminate our back log and stay caught up with our work?" At first I was concerned it wasn't going all that well. After we had a reasonable inventory of about twelve ideas, I asked everyone to vote for their top two choices. They were 1.) Hire more people, and 2.) Meet time standards. The second idea started to get me excited.

I decided to change directions at this point and have the group brainstorm answers to this question: "In what ways can we start meeting and exceeding our time standards?" After some logical and legitimate excuses for delays were mentioned, the meeting took off.

Excellent suggestions and discussions seemed to spontaneously occur. Many observations were brought up and discussed by members of the group. If I had lectured the group about these same observations, the ideas would have gone unheard. In fact, there is a good chance that I would have encountered a lot of defensiveness. When brought up by the group and discussed among themselves, the observations and suggestions hit home. There was ownership and responsibility.

I received more compliments from my group members on the quality of our meeting than I ever have before. In fact, I can't remember ever being complimented on a team meeting before.

The lesson I learned from this experience is that it is okay, in fact essential, that I be flexible and willing to improvise to achieve successful meetings that improve morale and get action.

Where are you and your team behind? Get your team together and have your own brainstorming session. Start by putting your issue in the "can"—use the word "can" when you write your questions: "In what ways can we . . . ?" If you persist, you will be surprised at the open, productive communication that results.

> *"It is a critical job of any entrepreneur to maximize creativity, and to build the kind of atmosphere that encourages people to have ideas. That means open structures, so that accepted thinking can be challenged."*
>
> Anita Roddick

Tips for Team Meetings

Try these tips for organizing and coaching a successful creative team meeting:

- Ask questions that are important to the group, and never allow one person to monopolize the discussion.
- Offer frequent positive feedback to individuals regarding their contributions to the team, but do this objectively. Saying "That's a good idea" is not objective: it reveals your evaluation of the idea, and you won't be able to say it about every idea. Saying "Thank you" does not imply your preference for one idea over another, and it encourages further participation.
- Stay on track by using the "parking lot." If an idea doesn't address the subject, park it in the "parking lot" by writing it on a separate flip chart page, and promise to address it later.
- Acknowledge individuals by name when listening to their ideas.
- Monitor non-verbal communication. Body language can tell a great deal about your progress. Watch for people stiffening up and crossing their arms and legs as though defending against attack.
- Provide interim summaries. This gives people the encouragement of hearing their own ideas again.
- Acknowledge the team's shared accomplishments and make sure that team members are aware of the impact of their ideas on solving the challenging issue. Give credit to the entire group, even after the brainstorming session.

Finding Space

Cheryl, a service supervisor for a dental equipment manufacturer, asked for her team's help to solve storage problems:

Our dental furniture warehouse needed more space. I explained the situation to my department and asked for their input. Someone suggested that we go out to the warehouse with a flip chart to brainstorm what could be eliminated, moved, disposed of, piled higher, or rearranged on our warehouse shelves.

We packed up our flip chart and moved from my office out to the warehouse floor. The brainstorming exercise only took about 30 minutes. To my surprise, we generated over 27 ideas from this short session!

We were able to implement at least 78 percent of the new ideas immediately. We are still working on the rest. All of them have merit. We found far more and far better ways to solve our problem than I thought possible.

The lesson I learned is that when I invest in brainstorming, my team and I are able to generate more ideas than just one or two of us working alone could even imagine. The more ideas we generate, the better ideas we have to work with. I found that through brainstorming, everyone takes ownership and becomes engaged.

Here is a question we ask the executive teams to consider when we conduct Turbo's Leadership Team Advance: "What, today, is impossible to do and, if you could do it, would revolutionize your business?" Try this question with your team.

One good way to brainstorm is to apply the idea-spurring questions developed by Dr. Alex Osborn in his book, *Applied Imagination.* By the time you have made the following four questions a habit—you will have already doubled your idea output.

1. Are there other uses for your idea or product?
2. Are there ways to adapt it?
3. Modify it?
4. Magnify it?[16]

Here are some examples of ways these questions have been expanded upon and answered.

1. Are there other uses for your idea or product?

- Is there a new way to use it as it is? (like a three-wheel motorcycle as a farm implement)
- Are there other ways it can be used if modified? (like a cover so you can use it in the rain)
- What could be made from this? (like ground up dollars made into "million dollar" paperweights)
- How about salvaging? (like turning old nuts, washers, and spark-plugs into art)

2. Adapt?

- What else is like this? (like a supercharged airplane is like a turbocharged car)
- What parallels does the past provide? (like the supercharger on the Auburn in 1937)
- Could other processes be copied? (hanging cars on a conveyor belt like sides of beef to make a production line)
- What other ideas might be adaptable? (like Diesel who got his engine ideas from a cigar lighter)

3. Modify?

- What other shape can we try? (like the buggy maker who tapered the roller bearing which Leonardo da Vinci had invented 400 years before)
- What other forms can we try? (like bath gel instead of bar soap)
- How can we create a new look? (like a box-shaped car)
- What could color do? (like pink and other pastels in automobiles to make 1955 one of the biggest new-car years in history)
- How about motion? (like seat belts that automatically lock)
- What about sound? (like the rotary engine that "hums" instead of going "ping, ping")

4. Magnify?

- Should we provide for a longer time? (like a 50,000-mile warranty)
- Should we offer with greater frequency? (like a 1962½ model Ford 500)
- Should we increase strength? (like reinforced heels and toes in hosiery)
- What about height? (like highboy 4 x 4 pickup trucks)

Get your team to ask these questions, then listen to validate their ideas and build an engaged team.

Actions for Engaging Leaders

- Don't give up on new idea generation.
- Whenever you are facing a problem, use green-light brainstorming.
- After you've made your brainstorming list, chunk it down, pick the number one idea on your list, and brainstorm again on the smaller pieces.
- Give full credit to your team for ideas that are generated.

Benefits You Will Gain

- Your problems will be solved.
- Your team members will be far more engaged.
- Everyone will buy into action plans.
- You will gain greater diversity of ideas.

"Do nothing ordinary."
Ralph Waldo Emerson

>>Principle 9

Dramatize Your Ideas

The 1994 Super Bowl between the San Francisco 49ers and the San Diego Chargers was a blow-out, and the commercials were as good as the game. For the first time there were awards for the best commercials. Remember the frogs on the lily pads saying "Bud – wise – rrrr, Bud – wise – rrrr, Bud – wise – rrrr"? The Rold Gold Pretzels man parachuting from the plane to the football field? The Pepsi machine that drew us in with the sound of the dollar bill being rejected? Monday, more people were talking about their favorite commercial than about the game.

What a dramatic combination. First, the commercials themselves were dramatic. Then, the network caused us to pay greater attention by having us choose our favorite, engaging us fully in the process. Take a lesson from the $4-million-per-30-second Super Bowl commercials: find a way to add drama to your presentation.

Merely stating a truth is not enough. Just presenting facts is not enough. When you talk about important matters, when you present your proposals, you need to sell your ideas. To do this, you must be more vivid and interesting—yes, even surprising. Showmanship: that's the ticket! The movies do it; television does it; so can you. Think about the most-viewed YouTube videos. Isn't part of their popularity due to their willingness to break with convention and do something different? Be creative! Arouse curiosity. Be unexpected and dramatic.

Red Sweater

John, president of the Portland Cement Company, is said to have gotten his start by using showmanship when he was a clerk at Armour's packing plant. Knowing that Mr. Armour had a habit of coming down to the plant very early in the morning, he came in early himself. Instead of the usual dress shirt and tie of the other clerks, he wore a red sweater.

One day Mr. Armour inquired, "Who is that?" John had caught the boss's attention—he was singled out from among all the other clerks. Now he had a chance to demonstrate his abilities. Once Mr. Armour was paying attention, he would soon see what an outstanding job John was doing.

Everyone Loves a Parade

On Saturday morning at about 7:00, we joined the overnight campers and the other early risers in anticipation of one of the nation's greatest displays of flowers, bands, and humanity: Portland's Rose Parade. Ultimately, 500,000 of us united to celebrate life, living, and being together.

Everyone loves a parade. My favorite part is the One-More-Time-Around Band. The band members, who average 40 years of age, are all former high school and college band members who love to get together once a year for the Rose Parade. They are so exuberant, so full of life!

Since we all love a parade, the action I call you to is to provide added value to your presentation by putting out a little something extra—the music to march to, the smile of a clown, the beauty of a princess. Like Donald Trump with his yachts and hotels, Liberace and his candelabra, the late Steve Jobs with his turtleneck and jeans at every Apple event, and Malcolm Forbes with his motorcycles, grab the other person's attention by doing something unexpected. These people were using showmanship—doing something new and different to astonish other people and arouse their curiosity. Gaining people's attention by expressing your point in novel and interesting ways, breaking the preoccupation of those you wish to engage with showmanship, can be a powerful leadership strategy.

Great Eight

I'll always remember the first time I stopped by Thomas Joseph's Personalized Dry Cleaning in Clackamas, OR. Mr. Joseph is passionate about his dry cleaning business. He's been featured in newspaper articles, photographed with Senators and the Blazers, and honored by his Rotary Club. As he showed me around his business, I was reminded that excellence, joy, passion, and fun are where you make them.

I first spotted Mr. Joseph carrying dry cleaning out to one of his customer's cars. I watched him as he greeted every customer by name as they walked into his store. Now wait until you read what he did with the announcement of his business's eighth anniversary:

> Let's celebrate! For **8** great years, you've depended on Thomas Joseph for his personalized dry cleaning services, and to celebrate the **8th** anniversary of Thomas Joseph's Dry Cleaning service, Thomas wants to say, "Thank you" in **8** great ways for **8** years of wonderful customers, with a special birthday party—Thursday, **8/8** and Friday, **8/9** from **8**:00 to **8**:00, come in for great cake and coffee. We can't wait to see you.

On it went, with eight ways, eight specials, all of which, of course, featured the number eight. Where did all of this creativity and innovation come from? It came from his team, as he likes to refer to the 16 people who work with him. Thomas sat down with his team and they brainstormed all of the great ways to play up the significance of the number eight. What a great use of showmanship to dramatize an idea. So why wait to be great? Sit up straight, mate. Take the bait. Look for and find eight ways to be great. It's not too late. You've got a date with fate!

Party Time

After completing 72 weeks of training for a paper mill, we had our graduation program. I didn't know we could have so much fun—balloons, whistles, poppers, pictures, and cake.

How do you view celebration? To celebrate is "to do something special or enjoyable for an important event, to mark with festivities or other deviation from routine to commemorate, with ceremony or festival, to break with normal business."[17] Think about one of your birthdays. Which one do you remember? It's probably the one you celebrated with gusto.

With celebration, you create a bond and you can consciously craft your culture. When you celebrate accomplishments and achievements, you anchor them and establish them as the new norm. You gain awareness. You become identified with your accomplishments; they become who you are. You see yourself as victorious. When you celebrate right, you acknowledge and empower yourself and others as winners. This builds engagement and esprit de corps, and you ready your team to win again.

"Ceremony is the smoke of friendship."
A Chinese proverb

Green Wallpaper

Breakthroughs happen in sales when a leader decides to do something out of the ordinary. Steve told me this fantastic story:

As the VP of sales and marketing for a salad dressing, pancake syrup, shortening, and oil company, one part of my job is attending annual food shows. This is where the manufacturers pay for a booth to exhibit their products. These shows have become profit centers for some distributors, who expect you to have greatly reduced prices with a buy-in, as well as spiff for the retailer or the distributor's salespeople. My challenge was to stimulate sales without losing profits.

After my first several shows as a manufacturer, I was feeling like a sucker until I hit on an idea to sell lots of products with a twist on the spiff money.

I ordered 100 sheets of uncut one-dollar bills from the Federal Mint. I bought tape, a rod, and some Plexiglas. Our booth was literally wall-to-wall money. We had a small sample table in front and bulk commodities visible in back. As people came by they would point at the sheets of money in the Plexiglas and ask, "Is this real?" "What are you selling?" "How much do I need to buy to get a half sheet of greenbacks?" By the end of the show my salesman and I had sold over five and a half truckloads of merchandise. People were carrying around our uncut bills almost like an advertising banner and talking to everyone about us and our booth.

When we took a break, we went to the restaurant across the street known for good food. With the other brokers and manufacturers, we sat at the bar waiting for a table. When we were called, I presented the payment to the bartender. He said, "This is about the twentieth time I have got this stuff tonight. Who is selling the money? It's illegal."

So I explained that the money was real and anyone can buy it from the U.S. Mint in sheets. It is illegal to deface or cut into the green part of a bill.

The next year at the same show, a woman who had previously bought twelve sheets worth of product came back to the show. I saw her come in. She made a beeline to my booth from the front door. "How much do I need to buy to get nineteen sheets of money?"

"Nineteen sheets!" I said. "You bought twelve sheets last year. Why do you want nineteen sheets?"

She said, "My husband and I papered our bathroom wall with the first twelve and we figure we need nineteen more to finish." Expensive wallpaper!

The upshot of all this was we won the best sales award at most of our shows this year, as well as the single booth award for the most unique idea.

Of course Steve won the award! He sold tons of product, amounts never before achieved, at a profit. But first he had to break out of conventional rut thinking. He had to dramatize his idea.

Part of dramatizing your idea is looking inside your organization to discover the people who have unusual ways of thinking. Look for those who are curious, who have an insatiable thirst for answers to the question about how things work and what can be done improve performance.

How do we stay curious and creative? And how do we keep our teams curious and creative? Remember: one of the places drama—doing things differently—comes from is the creative place. Hire curious people. Look for people who have consistently avoided the mainstream, who took a year off without pay to work in the inner city, kept bees as a hobby, set aside six weeks each year to travel abroad. If curiosity isn't on a person's resume, don't expect it to bloom tomorrow in your business.

The corollary is obvious: Don't hire conventional people. If they boast the solid gold resume (right school, right grades, right first job, and right year for first promotion), watch out.

"Measure" curiosity. When it's time for semi-annual performance reviews, consider having each employee submit a one-page essay on (a) the oddest thing I've done this year off the job, (b) the craziest idea I've tried at work, or (c) my most original screw-up, on the job or off. Using the answers to such questions, deal curiosity directly into the evaluation deck, near the top.

Change pace. Go to work next Thursday and declare it miniature-golf day. Showing a training film this afternoon? Order popcorn for every participant.

> *"The creative is the place where no one else has ever been. You have to leave the city of your comfort and go into the wilderness of your intuition. What you'll discover will be wonderful. What you'll discover will be yourself."*
>
> Alan Alda

Flying High

Alex, staff accountant for a local accounting firm, found that showing enthusiasm helped dramatize his idea. He told us,

About a month ago while I was on a flight home from San Diego, a great idea popped into my head. The idea was to create a process flowchart of how our clients' tax files flow through our office.

My intention was to create the flowcharts for our company first. As soon as we were competent and comfortable with the design, we could bundle the process flowcharts as an additional value-added client service offering. This idea would have tremendous upside for our company because it would be a new and innovative value-added offering for our entire client base.

I set up a meeting with my boss to discuss my idea. I was apprehensive about pitching my idea because he has nearly 30 years of public accounting experience. I was positive he had already thought of my idea and had dismissed it as being too costly and impractical. I thought about cancelling the meeting, but instead I pressed on with five times more enthusiasm.

When I presented the idea, I was energetic and upbeat with an emphasis on what it is, how it will work, and how it will create value for our clients and our firm. To my delight, he loved it! My boss allowed me to go forward with the idea, and now I am contributing to my company in a bigger way!

The lesson I learned from this experience is that enthusiastic presentation is a way of dramatizing my ideas, and when I enthusiastically dramatize my ideas, people love them.

Each of us is unique. The ideas that come to us may not come to anyone else in quite the same way. Don't assume your ideas have already been thought of by someone else. Alex thought of something that his boss, with over 30 years of experience, never had.

Good Night's Sleep

While traveling back from Idaho without an advance hotel reservation, I checked in at the Rugged Country Lodge in Pendleton, OR, a little hotel near the interstate. I had put in a long day, starting with an early breakfast meeting in Rexburg, ID, a midday meeting in Boise, and a dinner meeting in La Grande, OR. All I wanted now was a good night's sleep.

The first thing I noticed when I pulled in was the fresh paint and nice flowers planted around the parking lot. When I walked inside, the irresistible aroma of freshly baked cookies wafted through the lobby. I was greeted warmly by Gordon, the gentleman at the registration desk. After inquiring about the rate and asking to see a room, he and I continued our repartee. Gordon offered me fresh fruit, and milk to go with the cookies. Though I seldom eat cookies and never drink milk, I couldn't resist. What a treat! Gordon told me that a year ago, when the Wildhorse Resort & Casino opened with 500 rooms at the next exit east, it dramatically impacted their business. We talked a little longer, then I excused myself and went to my room.

The next morning, after enjoying their complimentary breakfast, I walked down to the office to check out. Gordon greeted me by name: "Good morning, Larry. Did you get a good rest?"

If I'm ever in Pendleton again near bedtime, I will stay at the Rugged Country Lodge, not because it's fancy, not because it's cheap. I'll stay because of their extraordinary customer service. It was genuine, warm, and Gordon's remembering my name the next morning dramatized his genuine interest in me.

Whether you have had another hotel built nearby with 500 rooms or not, you have a competitor of one kind or another chasing you. You must distinguish yourself by dramatizing your desire to provide a superior customer experience or you will end up selling to your competitor or, worse, hanging up a closed sign. There are no other choices.

What is your cookies and milk? What are the extra-mile, extra-value services you can provide that will give your clients the feeling of being special without eroding your profits? The people who can tell you are not that far away—your service department, your delivery people, your internal customer service team—all you have to do is ask. You could go direct and ask your customers. You may be amazed at how little is required for you to add the special value that will set you apart, give you a competitive edge. Ask your team the question, "How can we serve our customers at ever higher levels to earn their business today and their repeat business tomorrow?"

Oakland A's

Change the pace is what Juliana, Nordstrom's northern California regional manager, did when she announced to her thirty department managers that she had arranged a visit to the company's distribution center and they should wear their jeans and sneakers the following day.

She asked them to meet her at 10 a.m. at her Walnut Creek store, where a chartered bus would be waiting to pick up everybody. When the bus started off in the direction of Oakland, CA, instead of the distribution center, the managers became suspicious. Their suspicions turned to joy and surprise when the bus arrived at the Oakland A's stadium. To dramatize her appreciation, Juliana had arranged box seats for her team of managers who ate hot dogs, drank soft drinks, and had an unscheduled vacation day at company expense.

This is how you build collective loyalty and engagement. Give your team a surprise and you will be surprised by the renewed commitment the team members bring back to their jobs after you've demonstrated that you care enough to do something special for them.

Actions for Engaging Leaders

- Find a reason to celebrate.
- Share your ideas with upbeat animation.
- Ask customers what extra-mile value you could offer.

Benefits You Will Gain

- Your celebration will serve as a turbo thrust.
- You will sell your ideas with greater ease.
- You will increase customer interest and loyalty.

"Excitement is impossible where there is no contest."
Henry Cabot Lodge

>>>Principle 10

Stimulate Competition

Sharon, office manager for a beverage distributor, had been talking with her supervisor about morale in their office. They began brainstorming ideas to spark their staff's enthusiasm. Sharon suggested trying a new and different incentive. She told us,

> We wanted the office staff to get out and see what the salesmen and drivers are faced with every day as they make sales and service calls, so we created a retail sales incentive program. After deciding on the specifics of the program, Tom and I presented it to the general manager, who approved wholeheartedly.
>
> I told the office staff about the promotion, and we formed teams to present our incentive program to small retail accounts that were not presently buying our products, and we challenged each other to see who could get the most accounts. My team partner Maxine and I went out first because I had some sure buys to get the team's adrenaline going and bolster their belief that we could do it.
>
> When we came back with four placements the first day, everyone was excited. As teams went out on sales calls, the excitement and the challenge to win the

competition grew. After two weeks, we had placed 35 new products in previously inactive accounts.

The whole company was buzzing about our success, and our inside office team was elated. Morale was at an all-time high. We still laugh about how scared we were and our amateur sales pitches!

A great way to get things done and enhance job satisfaction is to stimulate competition with the challenge of a contest. Money alone does not bring good people together, nor does it hold them together. Exciting ideas do! It is the game itself—the opportunity to excel and prove worth, the chance to win—that brings and holds teams together. That's what makes marathons, triathlons, chess tournaments, and multi-player video games exciting: the desire to excel and earn that winning feeling.

Here's a way you can help your enterprise become more competitive and be more than ordinary. Don't add to the workload. Instead, increase the challenge. Sharon's example shows that better morale, engagement, and success can result from adding more challenge to the job. When done well, this kind of "job enhancement" is empowering and engaging.

Try Out

When Leslie encounters a team member who needs some extra encouragement to get in the game, she remembers a time when she was challenged by her parents to go outside her comfort zone to pursue something she loved. She told us,

During the summer between my junior and senior year in high school, my dad got transferred from Wyoming to Southern California. The school I attended in Thermopolis, WY, had about 350 students in the whole school. I was in for a culture shock! I spent most of my senior year keeping to myself. There were just way too many people. I didn't know anyone. I was used to being the "popular kid," the great athlete. In

Thermopolis, I was a starter for volleyball, basketball, and softball. I had a reason to go to school. I loved it and everyone loved me. When I got to California, it was too late to go out for volleyball, and by the time basketball tryouts came around, I just wanted to go "home" to Wyoming, so I didn't try out.

When softball tryouts were announced, I had an excuse for every argument my parents gave for why I should try out. They tried for two weeks to get me to go to tryouts and I held my ground. They put my equipment on my bed; I put it back in the box. They put my trophies and awards out on my dresser; I put them back in the drawer. After all, my misery was "their fault" for moving me to this place.

The day of tryouts came, and much to my surprise, when I got into my car to drive to school, all of my softball gear was on the passenger side of my car with a note from my mom with four big bold words on it: "YOU WILL REGRET IT." I thought about that all day. I guess that was the challenge I needed. When school got out, I went to the tryouts.

After two days of tryouts, the list was posted and I had made the team. All of a sudden, girls that had ignored me were my friends. Practices began and I became a starter before the first game. We only lost two games all year and won the California state championship. I wanted a redo on my senior year.

The lesson I learned from this experience is to not give up on my potentially strong team player who may be intimidated by the challenge of a larger game.

USA Today Headline

Shelley, supervisor for a restaurant chain in Yakima, WA, prepared her team to compete. She told us,

When I returned from vacation, my boss called me into her office to tell me the company had just

145

terminated fifteen employees in one of our restaurants. She wanted me to take over that restaurant and get it back on track.

In addition to the challenge of recharging this restaurant that had just experienced a major crisis, there was a national "Super Saturday" contest coming up in two months that we needed to prepare for. "Super Saturday" is where we price products extra low for one day to drive up customer count and introduce new products. We use "Super Saturday" to break the routine and prove how well we can function as a team.

I began immediately with back-to-basics training on all the high-performance activities: food quality, speed of service, and all of our customer service elements.

After two months of training, coaching, and pumping up the team, they did it! They were in the top 2 percent of all USA McDonald's restaurants in the contest. In fact, our Ellensburg restaurant was listed in an article that appeared in *USA Today*. My crew was rewarded with prizes and a wonderful celebration party.

Most important, our team felt a sense of pride and accomplishment that only hard work, accompanied by celebrated success can bring. During the training months that led up to "Super Saturday," our sales increased 8 percent. We finished the month of the contest up 11.1 percent in sales. These are big numbers for us.

The lesson I learned from this experience is that the challenge of a contest with stretch goals, accompanied by the training needed, builds belief, and the results often exceed any of our highest expectations.

Star

When I was conducting a training session for Boise Cascade at the Red Lion Inn. A young server came into our room at break time with a tub of soft drinks. I noticed a little blue stick-on star (the kind you might get at Sunday school) on his name tag. "Howard," I asked, "what is the blue star for?"

He answered, "Oh, the star? We're having a safety contest. We're trying to see who can be the safest this quarter. We formed teams and my team was the safest last month. That's why I have a blue star. If we win, we get an award."

"What is the award if you win?"

"I don't know," he said, "I think it's a pizza."

Howard wasn't sure what the award was going to be, but he was motivated by the challenge of the contest.

One of your challenges is to find a way to lessen the boredom when your team's jobs consist of routine, mundane tasks. Give them new, creative challenges. Up the challenge, not the workload—a challenge that allows for personal growth. This challenge will motivate your team members and they will become more fully engaged.

If you want to engage your team with a contest, be sure there are ways to have immediate wins. When the wins come, celebrate your successes. Celebration provides the afterburner effect that will turbo-charge your team's performance.

Dictator to Cheerleader

Sylvia told us she learned the importance of providing a meaningful incentive when she gave her team a challenge:

> I became the local facility manager for a national gas station and convenience store chain. I had been a restaurant manager for the previous eight years, but didn't know anything about fuel stations or convenience stores. Taking over a store that was not doing well was quite a struggle, especially since I felt I didn't know what I was doing. It took about two years for the station to start making profits and for the employees to get on board doing the right things to help grow the business.

The company had a mystery shopper program. Twice a month, a secret shopper would come in, purchase items, asks questions, and check out our facility for customer service and cleanliness. The company wanted to ensure every store was adhering to their standards. No one in the store knew who the person was or when they were coming until we got our score.

The corporation had a nationwide contest. The winning managers from the top-performing stores got a trip to Las Vegas for an all-expense paid week of company celebrations. They would get to go to shows, fancy dinners, and mixers with other managers from the company.

In 2004, I decided I was going to win the trip to Vegas. To qualify, we had to get all 24 mystery shop scores of 90 percent or better. At the beginning of the year, I sat with my team and told them we were *going* to win this year's mystery shop reward. They all knew what to do, how to do it, and we were *going* to do it.

In March, we got an 83 percent and our chances of winning were gone. January 2005 came and I sat down with my team, *told* them we were *going* to win the mystery shop award, and if we didn't score 90 percent on a mystery shop, there would be consequences.

The first four months were wonderful. We were averaging 94 percent mystery shop scores. I was elated, and then in May, 87 percent. Another year, no Vegas.

As I sat with my team again in January 2006, I tried something new. I asked them what we could do as a team to get the mystery shop award. They thought they were doing everything right and didn't think there was anything else they could do—we either won or we didn't. I noticed a lot of ambivalence towards MY award.

Then a member of my team said those famous words, *"What's in it for us?"* They were right; I was going to

Vegas, they would stay home and work. We sat for an extra hour that day brainstorming ideas of how they would benefit, how I could make it as important to them as it was to me. Their ideas worked. *We* won the award with a yearly mystery shop average score of 93.87 percent.

The lesson I learned from this experience is that I have to make the challenge, the contest, about the team, not about me and what I want or need. There must be rewards and benefits for the team, incentives that are meaningful to them.

Don't miss this important point when constructing your incentives. What will your team value most, enjoy most, appreciate most? Do they want a golf or paintball outing, a picnic or a night at the movies, a cash incentive or a day off?

CUZ

When the subject of stimulating competition came up, Duane shared a fun idea:

At our September managers' meeting, we brainstormed the question, "In what ways can we improve customer service?" We developed a multitude of ideas and ultimately landed on a program we decided to call CUZ (Customer "Uwareness" Zone). Our goals were to improve customer awareness, in-house customer service, and, ultimately, sales.

We defined the Customer "Uwareness" Zone as the ten-foot radius around the customer. The goal was to ensure that all customer service personnel, stockers, and managers said, "Hello," paid attention to customers, and, when appropriate, asked to help them. When and if one of our employees caught a manager not living up to the CUZ pledge by failing to greet a customer within ten feet, the employee was instructed to tap them on the shoulder and say "CUZ."

Each manager was given a stock of CUZ slips to give to employees that caught them neglecting a customer. Each CUZ slip was worth 50 cents toward a surprise at our annual fall Halloween luncheon. At the end of the month, each store manager reported at our managers' meeting the number of times they had been caught and the number of slips they had given out.

As of now, the leading store has given out only six CUZ slips. What this has done for our customer service awareness has been almost unbelievable, and, in terms of increased sales, we have just completed the best fall season in the history of our 35-year-old firm. We have actually had customers asking if our employees are on a commission.

The lesson I learned is that by throwing down a challenge—introducing a little friendly, fun competition—people will change their behavior. Friendly, fun competition can go a long way toward creating enhanced esprit de corps, greater customer awareness, and, in our case, increased sales and profits.

Pedal to the Metal

Chris, general manager for a local mechanical contracting company, found that meeting a challenge in one area of his life energized him to accomplish more in other areas. He told us,

> About the time we started this class, my cycling time was in decline. The time commitment required for the LDL (I ride mostly in the evenings), coupled with other obligations of my personal time, became an excuse for why I wasn't riding as much as I would have liked. Once I started down this path of excuses, it compounded: the less I rode, the more strength I lost and the less I wanted to get on my bike, because I knew it would be hard work.
>
> In Session 7, we were asked to create a new three-week goal. This was just the push I needed to get myself back on the bike. I announced to the entire class that I

was going to ride 300 miles in the next three weeks—something I had never done before!

I started the first week riding shorter distances of around 20 miles, ramping up to 32 to 35 miles in the second week. During this challenge, I set 14 personal records and checked off an item from my summer bucket list—I commuted to work, a round trip of 74 miles.

Yesterday morning, I sent my wife a text telling her that I had just completed my 300-mile goal. And I was still ten miles from home. My three-week total ended up at 310.5 miles! Even though the challenge is over and I will be on vacation next week, I am now committed to 400 miles by the end of this month.

Over the last three weeks, I learned some things about myself. Not only could I make enough time to achieve this one goal, I fit in several others as well. I painted my house and stained the deck (with the help of my wife), cleaned out the garage, cleaned my shop, removed an unwanted shed from my yard, and performed a number of other small maintenance tasks around our home.

What I have learned is that when I procrastinate, I need an outside force, the challenge of committing to a goal, to get me going. I learned that once I get moving, it is hard to stop me.

> *"A body at rest tends to remain at rest.*
> *A body in motion tends to remain in motion."*
> Isaac Newton

New World's Record

Ray, service manager for a well-established tire and re-tread company, told us,

A few weeks ago, one of my servicemen dismounted 147 tires and mounted 43 additional tires. I created an

8½ x 11-inch poster using my word document program that read, "Ricardo, The King – New World's Record – Thank You for Your Hard Work." I put the poster on our bulletin board near the time clock where everyone would see it. The response of other service team members was, "We can do that much in half the time!"

It's nice to have this kind of friendly competition. The stimulus worked so well that in April, our service team set a new "world's record" of $107,000 in billable service labor. Once again, I put up a poster recognizing the team for their accomplishments. I also brought in pizza for the whole team. Each week I take down the old posters and hang up new posters that praise and recognize the team for their achievements, regardless of the size.

The lesson I learned from this experience is that when I stimulate competition and provide recognition, I create the winning combination of improved productivity, enhanced esprit de corps, and increased teamwork.

Who are the winners in this story? The answers are pretty obvious: customers didn't have to wait as long, so that's a win, and the company was able to reduce their labor costs as a percentage of sales while improving their performance and efficiency—that's a win. And team members experienced a greater sense of accomplishment—that's a win.

Here's another question: could they have delivered this level of outstanding performance, this "world's record" level of performance, and failed to experience the sense of accomplishment Ray spoke of? The answer may not be as obvious. It's "yes." Your job as an engaging leader is to recognize the contribution, the achievement, the performance of your team members and celebrate it, draw attention to it, have fun with it. Do this and you will create a high-performance team that will outdo their bests and continually improve. With continuing improvement, everyone will grow. You will maximize the value of your most important resource, your human resource, and *you* will be a winner.

> *"When healthy competition prevails,*
> *you come out to play and you play to win."*
> Lorii Myers

Walk On

Marcella, HR specialist for a food distribution company in WA, was challenged by her father to be persistent in the face of discouragement. Her persistence paid off. She told us,

> In my senior year of high school, I decided not to take any of the athletic scholarships I was offered so I could stay close to home and attend the University of Washington. My dad encouraged me to walk on to the basketball team because he felt I could do it, so I did try out during my freshman year. I was given 30 minutes in a scrimmage to showcase my ability. Afterwards, the coach told me they really didn't take walk-ons and he only let me try out to satisfy NCAA regulations.
>
> That spring the team had a coaching change; someone new was in charge. My dad once again urged me to walk on. What was the worst that could happen— I wouldn't make it again? I spoke with the coach and began preseason conditioning with the team. This time I was given a two-week tryout. I made the team and had a full-ride scholarship for the next three years.
>
> The lesson I learned from this experience is that all it takes is one person to throw down the challenge.

I love this story. It's an amazing story about many things, including the power of persistence, the willingness to try again, the willingness to come back and ask one more time when you've already been told "No" in no uncertain terms. I love this story because it's a story of the power of a coach, a challenging, caring, concerned coach—in this case, a dad who's willing to exercise more belief in his daughter than his daughter had in herself. That's your job as a coach: to give your team that extra challenge and encouragement so they will try one more time, even when they feel they've been told a final "No." And you know what you gain: engagement and excellence—a winning team!

There will always be people standing on the sidelines saying, "Look at how lucky she is," "Look at how lucky he is." They will never understand until they learn from personal experience, until they give it a try themselves, the power of persistence, the power of trying one more time, even when we're told "No," even when we're told it's impossible. So I challenge you to ask once again when you've been turned away. I further challenge you to be the leader who urges someone on, the one who gives them that extra stimulus.

Actions for Engaging Leaders

- Create a little friendly competition for your team.
- Apply the outside force of committing to a goal.
- Keep and publish your scores.

Benefits You Will Gain

- You will have the joy of watching your team grow.
- You will set performance records.
- Your level of excellence will rise.
- Your team will go the extra mile.
- You may have your best year ever.

"Perfect is the enemy of good."
Voltaire

>>>Principle 11

When You Blow It, Show It

Dave took his set of blueprints to a new job site. When he opened up the prints to begin familiarizing himself with the project, the most important blueprint was missing.

He called back to his office. "Where is the main project print?" he asked.

His office called the project design people: "Where is the blueprint?"

"Nothing here. You have it."

"No, you must have it!"

A day later, still no blueprint. Three days later, still no blueprint. Everything was up in the air. Dave kept calling: "It's going to be hard to do this job right without *all* the blueprints."

On the fourth day, Dave was looking through some of his drawings, and there, to his amazement, was the missing blueprint. He had had the print the whole time!

Wow, was he embarrassed! What to do? We know the right answer: Call the office immediately and admit the mistake. We also know other possible answers: Hide it; throw it away; sneak it back to the office so it looks like it was always there. We can be so creative when it comes to covering up our mistakes!

If we wish to create an empowered, engaged team, we must allow people the space and grace to be honest. To Dave's credit, that's what he did. He called his office and admitted that he had had the print the whole time—and *he* had misplaced it.

As engaging leaders, what should our attitude be toward mistakes? First, let's break the word down: miss-takes—like in the film business. Our middle son, Barry, owned a video production company. When he was shooting a commercial or training video and the first take wasn't successful, he'd shoot a second take, a third take, and so on. There is no blame, shame, or attempt to shift responsibility.

High performance companies have a similar attitude toward mistakes. They have learned to allow for, and even encourage, mistakes—especially mistakes that are inevitable while in the pursuit of break-through, performance-improving innovations. Unless there is an atmosphere that allows for mistakes, there will be no risk taking, and we may even create an atmosphere where people abandon their commitment to honesty. Continuous improvement will be replaced by cover ups and finger pointing. The driving force, the cultural norm, will be "Keep your head down," "Play it safe."

What role does "when you blow it, show it" play in engaging leadership? The answer: a profound role. One of your main assignments as an engaging leader is to build trust. When you make mistakes and are willing to admit it, you are showing vulnerability. The willingness to be vulnerable is at the heart of building trust.

If you try to create a culture that does not allow for mistakes, doesn't permit people to get something wrong, and is overly harsh when people stumble, you create a culture that holds back, is tentative, masterful at cover-up and dodging accountability and responsibility, a culture that takes no risks, an organization where little improvement occurs. Everyone becomes good at "blame-storming," skillful at pointing out the mistakes of others. You will never secure full engagement in a world that requires perfection.

Pane Pain

Kelly told us that after going to work as a commercial glass installer, he was assigned the job of placing windows in the remodel of the Montgomery Park Building in Portland, OR. As he was moving the long, heavy boxes up the scaffolding to work on top of the structure four stories in the air, he heard the gut-wrenching sound of glass breaking. He struggled to get control of the falling boxes—too late. Eleven windows were broken—a loss of material and time, potentially creating a scheduling bottleneck.

When Kelly reluctantly called the office to relate what had happened, he first heard some laughter, and then the words, "Accidents happen. Don't worry about it, just keep moving. We have extra windows in stock."

The lesson I learned from this example is that capable leaders are prepared for the inevitable breakdowns that occur as we move toward our objectives. They don't over-dramatize the mistakes. They expect and are prepared for a few mistakes along the way.

Pilings

Dee, a senior project engineer, spent many hours and concentrated effort laying out a detailed project plan for one of his young, self-assured project engineers. Then Dee went over the plan in detail. When they were finished, Dee felt he had eliminated any possibility for misunderstanding.

The project had been in progress for a couple of days when the owner's survey crew showed up to inspect. They discovered the entire dry-dock was nine feet from where the plans specified.

The owner's representative called Dee, who jumped in his pickup and rushed over to take a look. Sure enough, the structure was in the wrong place.

"I was biting my tongue," Dee said. "I wanted to say, 'How could you be so stupid? How could you possibly make a mistake like this?'"

Dee told us that a few years earlier, he had fired someone on the spot for this kind of mistake. This time, he and this young project engineer modified the plan to make things work.

As is often the case, they were able to find a way that worked—a plan that made the owner happy and didn't cost any extra money.

When Dee returned to the job site a day later, there was a lot of kidding going on. When the project engineer went over to get his pickup truck, someone said, "Better be careful with that. If you drive nine feet to the left, you'll end up in the river." Dee encouraged the crew to lighten up.

He told us his project engineer was working harder than ever, had a good attitude, and was putting his heart and head into the job. "If I had lost my temper or fired this guy, it would have been a far bigger mistake than the project engineer's mistake of putting the pilings in the wrong place," Dee said. "His mistake cost us a little time and credibility. If I had fired him, it would have cost our firm a great deal in lost time, lost training, and experience."

He added, "The lesson I learned is when my intention is to build people and make them successful, I don't need to rub it in when they make a mistake. What I need to do is help them save face, learn from their experience, and move on."

Admit It

I watched a young man stand in front of the Leadership Development Lab and talk about the frustrating relationship he has with his ex-wife. He hadn't wanted the divorce in the first place, and they were becoming more and more distant as time passed. Finally, he asked her if they could talk about what was causing the distance between them

She said, "You've never admitted you were wrong."

As he told this story, he had a difficult time saying, "I admitted I was wrong." In fact, he couldn't say, "I admitted I was wrong," until I asked him to say those exact words. When he did, his face changed. The wrinkles in his brow smoothed out, the crow's feet in the corners of his eyes went away, and a smile came over his face. I watched this young man, who had been hiding behind pride and fear, begin to experience the power and confidence, the release that comes when we simply say, "I was wrong."

Take full responsibility for every decision you make. Never blame others for the things that go wrong that are your responsibility. Be willing to say, "I was wrong." Taking this courageous stance will set the example for others to be as courageous, humble, transparent, and as coachable as you. You can waste a lot of time and energy trying to cover up your mistakes. When you willingly admit errors in judgment, action, and performance, it relieves tension and you win respect. You set the standard for appropriate professional behavior for others to follow.

Hang In There

Mark, supervisor for a Clark County commercial plumbing contractor, didn't have to admit a mistake, but was glad he did. He told us,

Mike, one of my crew members, was struggling to support some cast iron pipe in a wall. I immediately jumped in with a "Let me show you how to do that." As he watched, I did it with a lot less effort and time than it was taking him. I was proud of myself and said, "There you go," then walked away.

159

I had walked about 100 feet when it hit me. "Ah, crap! I forgot to use Turbo's 3-Step On-the-Job Training Process."[18] Instead, I just did it and walked away. As I thought about it, I could tell that when I hung the pipe for him, he really didn't understand what I was doing and he was a little frustrated with me.

So I turned around, marched back, and apologized to Mike for my behavior. I asked him if I could share some of what I have been learning. He agreed, so I shared how I'm supposed to use the 3-Step On-the-Job Training Process instead of my old habit of just doing it. I asked him if we could try it to train him in how to easily install supports for the cast iron pipe. He humored me, and we went through the three steps: trainer says / trainer does; trainer says / trainee does; trainee says / trainee does.

By the end of the three steps—it took a few minutes—we were both laughing and joking with each other. Only a few minutes before, there had been tension because I didn't use the opportunity to make this situation a "teaching moment." This time when I walked away, I left behind an empowered team member who has more respect for me and for himself. I built rapport with him, and he can now perform one of his basic functions at a much higher level of efficiency.

The lesson I learned from this experience is to own up to my mistakes and to ask for forgiveness when I blow it."

> *"Failure is the opportunity to*
> *begin again more intelligently."*
> Henry Ford

Up to Your Neck in It

Sometimes your mistakes can serve as learning tools for others. Mark was the area coordinator for a paper machine trial. His crew was testing a vendor's new additives. The vendor told Mark they might run out of the additive and be forced to shut down the trial. Mark went to investigate. While standing on the platform above the tank containing the additive, he noticed it was running low. As he was leaning over with a tape measure trying to get an accurate measurement of the remaining supply, the platform collapsed and he fell into the tank. Mark now makes a strong point for following all safety procedures by using his own example of blowing it.

My Wife Was Right

A remarkable example of how to admit a mistake—in this case an error in judgment—was demonstrated by Tom Peterson, an iconic retailer in the Portland area, who, after 25 years, filed for bankruptcy. Against his wife's advice, he had bought Stereo Super Stores, and this decision was disastrous. He ran a full page notice in the *Oregonian*:

> I'm in trouble.
> I have been forced to take Chapter 11
> reorganization in the Courts.
> I made a mistake.
> I should have listened to my wife.
> She said, "Don't buy Stereo Super Stores;
> it won't work." She was right.
> I've been successful before.
> I can be successful again,
> but I'll need your help.
>
> Whatever you need in TVs, Stereos,
> Furniture and Appliances, please buy today.
> Our prices have always been right;
> they're even better now!
> I promise you the same friendly
> customer service you deserve and expect.
> My family and I want to extend
> our personal thanks to the hundreds
> of customers who responded last week.

Tom Peterson's very public admission that he had blown it earned him a good deal of admiration and customer trust.

Be a risk taker when it comes to trust. Letting people know where you stand on important issues is a risky proposition because you can't be certain that others will appreciate your candor, agree with your aspirations, or interpret your message the way you intended. But unless you're willing to be open, you can't expect others to take the same risk necessary to build trust.

Being open also extends to acknowledging your own mistakes. Some people fear that by admitting mistakes they'll lose respect and power. Experience shows that letting others know you are human is one of the best ways to enhance your credibility. People tend to distrust those who claim to be infallible. I'm not suggesting that you reveal your every fault; I do strongly recommend that you admit when you're wrong and let others know you are approachable.

Overdrawn

The comptroller of a construction firm in Seattle told us that as she was balancing the accounts, she was astonished to discover that the company was overdrawn. She knew the company had a credit line but didn't like to tap into it. She felt she had no choice but to immediately go into the president's office and tell him what she'd discovered. She and the president called the bank to research their account.

We all love a story with a happy ending, and this story has one. As it turns out, the bank had made a mistake; they had blown it. The comptroller grew in the president's estimation and enhanced his trust in her because she immediately reported the overdraft instead of running around trying to cover it up or solve the problem by herself. "When You Blow It, Show It" not only helps you save face with others in the long term, it helps you save a tremendous amount of personal stress and enables you to maintain your integrity.

Wrong Format: Right Response

Honesty about mistakes almost always results in praise from the person we tell. Carolyn told us a story about her frustrated boss bringing some documents into her office which he thought one of Carolyn's staff members had prepared. In a disgusted way, he threw it on her desk and said, "Would you please tell so-and-so that this is not the format I want in the future!"

He left the office. Carolyn looked at what he'd put on her desk and realized it was work that *she* had prepared. She was then faced with a decision—a decision not unlike the decisions you and I are faced with from time to time, a decision which tests our character. Carolyn hesitated, then picked up the documents, walked into her boss's office and said, "I'm sorry. I need to tell you that I'm the one who did this work."

Of course her boss was surprised and impressed that she was so forthright and honest. Carolyn went a long way toward strengthening her credibility with her boss and empowering her team with her honest admission of her mistake.

> *"Those who can own up to their own errors are greater than those who merely know how to avoid making them."*
> Cardinal DeRetz

On the Level

Kelly, project manager for a mechanical contractor, made the decision to always own up to his mistakes when he encountered someone who didn't. He told us,

> In my second year of apprenticeship while working for Wright Shuchart and Harbor in Longview, WA, I was given a wonderful opportunity to broaden my skillset. One week, we were trained on levels and transit.

The following week, as we were getting ready to set up for some shots, the foreman became distracted in conversation. I decided to set up the instrument for him. When he checked it, it was perfect, so he decided to teach me how to do the surveys and layouts.

Within a couple of months, I was the chief surveyor for a $48 million dollar project! Weeks later, we were laying out anchor bolts for pulp tanks on the other side of the project. It was stressful. As we set the bolts, the concrete trucks were pouring; imagine being on the inside of a double rebar matt as the concrete is coming towards you!

I had my state-of-the-art Wild Theodolite instrument, complete with optical plumb, set up in a ribboned-off area to protect my survey hub. It was an expensive unit, costing upwards of $10,000 dollars.

I needed to go check the prints to confirm a calculation. When I came back, I couldn't see through the instrument. The lens was completely shattered and lying on the ground. The adjustment plate was bent at an odd angle. It was apparent that the instrument had gone down hard. I went directly to the office to report what had happened.

When the project manager, an old Russian fella named Val, came to the job site. I said, "I was setting the bolts at the HI Tank, went to my print, and when I came back, the Theodolite was toast—knocked over and set back in place." All he heard was that the Theodolite had gone over. He swore and shouted, "NEXT TIME ONE OF THOSE GOES DOWN, I WANT YOU UNDER IT AND I WANT BLOOD!"

I felt crushed! As he was walking away, he stopped, took a moment to reflect, gave me a wink and a smile, telling me it would be alright.

At the end of the pour, the concrete pump operator came over to tell me what had happened. He told me the labor foreman had backed a concrete truck up next to my instrument, let go of the chute, and the chute had swung into my instrument, knocking it down. When I asked the labor foreman about this, he said he didn't know what I was talking about.

The lesson I learned from this experience is that I never want to be someone who lies about my mistakes. I want to have integrity and honor as I go through life; to look forward, not backward; to own up to my actions and when I blow it, do what I can to make it right. When my team members make mistakes, I tell them, "It is not our mistakes that define us; it is how we respond when we blow it.

Is there room for you to have a lighter touch with the mistakes of your team and to be more courageous in admitting your own mistakes? If we accept that mistakes are expected steps toward product and service improvement, then there should be no need to hide them. They should be acknowledged so everyone can learn from them.

Actions for Engaging Leaders

- Never try to cover up your mistakes.
- Admit your errors in judgment and performance.
- Create an atmosphere of grace in your workplace.

Benefits You Will Gain

- You'll win respect.
- You'll relieve tension.
- You'll set the standard for a professional response to mistakes.

"He who argues is not a good man."

Lao-tzu

>>>Principle 12

Avoid Dogmatic Declarations

David, a project manager in Seattle, told us about a problem between the sheet metal installer for a mechanical contractor and the rest of the subcontractors on an important project at the University of Washington.

The sheet metal contractor told David, "The parts I need to shield the lights have not come in and won't be in for 90 days." He went on to say, "We can't finish our part of the project. We've done all we can for now. We'll just have to wait for three months until the parts come in, then we can finish up the job."

This dogmatic declaration on the part of the sheet metal contractor put David, the other subcontractors, and the rest of the crew in a bind. David felt like saying, "I can't believe you! How can you possibly block the entire project? This is just an excuse. You haven't looked for an alternate plan. There has to be another alternative!"

Instead, David gave the situation some thought over the weekend. On Monday, he called a meeting of all the contractors on the project.

"We have a problem," he said. He went on to describe the problem (no light shields) in impartial, dispassionate terms, then he said, "We need to finish this project on schedule. Now how can we complete on schedule without the light shields?"

He put the question to everyone on the job who had any impact on the project.

"I'd like to meet again with all the subcontractors, owners, and engineers on Wednesday," David said. Then he turned to the sheet metal contractor and said, "I'd like for you to be there and tell us your ideas for solving the problem."

To David's amazement, the sheet metal contractor showed up at the Wednesday meeting with a great idea, an idea that would solve the light shield problem. It was an answer the sheet metal contractor was committed to, a solution that met the core requirements. David got everyone's agreement and buy-in to the modified plan. The project was completed successfully and on time.

Dogmatic declarations say, in effect, "I have decided. There is nothing more to say on the subject. I have all the answers. Your ideas are not welcome or needed." Dogmatic declarations slam the door of receptivity. They stop forward movement. They stop improvement and innovation. They make others defensive and reduce understanding, cooperation, and creativity. Do not make dogmatic declarations to prove who's boss. If you have to prove who's boss, you are not. Remember: people, like boats, toot loudest when they're in a fog.

Olives Observer

Dogmatic declarations can have the effect of focusing people's attention on minor issues. Our son Larry Jr., who owns several sandwich shops, says, "If a restaurant operator is so worried about food costs that she starts dictating how many olives the 'sandwich artist' uses, that's where everyone's focus is. Instead of focusing on speed and service, which will improve sales, now conserving olives is all anyone is paying attention to. When sales go up, costs as a percentage of sales goes down. Olives just aren't that important!"

How are you directing the attention of your team? If they're focused on minor cost details, it's possible you've made some dogmatic declarations about those very things.

Dried Up

Derra, office manager for a Longview trucking company, was frustrated by a dogmatic declaration at home. She and her husband were sitting in the living room of their home in Kelso, WA. Suddenly, they were shocked by a screeching sound they heard coming from the other end of the house.

They jumped up, ran down the hall to the utility room, and discovered their clothes dryer making the unmistakable grinding noise of a dry, burned-out bearing. Derra turned it off in disgust. That night they bemoaned the fact that they would have to buy a new dryer. They didn't know where the money was going to come from.

The next morning, Derra decided to take it apart and fix it herself. She had the make and model number of the machine and location of the bearing written down for Don before he got up. She asked him to pick up the bearing they needed on his lunch hour. He said it was ridiculous for her to try to fix it and was upset that she had gone ahead and taken the dryer apart. He wanted them to just bite the bullet and buy a new dryer.

Derra first felt deflated and disappointed. Then she got angry. She thought repairing the dryer was an option worth at least discussing and didn't like Don's swift declaration that her idea was "ridiculous."

Fortunately, Derra and Don resolved their disagreement. They might have gotten their clothes dry sooner if Don had avoided making dogmatic declarations. He could have said, "What are the steps involved in fixing it?"

And Derra could have discussed her idea with Don before taking the dryer apart. Sometimes taking preemptive action can have the same effect as a dogmatic declaration. Taking action before discussing it with fellow team members leaves your team with few or no options, and it can lead to disempowerment and disengagement.

Blind and Blindest

Sarcasm can be another way to camouflage dogmatic declarations, Denis, operating supervisor for a paper mill in northern Ontario, Canada, told us,

> When I returned to work after a long, painful, debilitating eye illness, which resulted in me losing 100 percent of my vision in one eye and 50 percent of my vision in the other eye, my boss asked me, "How did you enjoy your little vacation?"

> I was outraged at his audacity. My disgusted reply to his sarcastic question was, "If you think going blind in one eye and losing 50 percent of your vision in the other eye is a vacation, clearly you're an idiot." I turned around, left the room, and went straight to my office. From that day forward, our working relationship has been strained. I lost a lot of respect for my boss.

> The lesson I learned from this experience is that there is no place for sarcasm in the workplace. What one person may think of as being amusing, cute, or clever could be extremely personal and hurtful to another.

Notice that Denis's supervisor didn't ask him an honest question. If you don't ask an honest question, you haven't invited an honest answer or an open, honest conversation. Like a dogmatic declaration, a sarcastic question shuts down the conversation.

According to the Oxford English Dictionary, "sarcasm" comes from the ancient Greek *sarkasmos* meaning "to tear flesh." Merriam-Webster Online defines sarcasm as "the use of words that mean the opposite of what you really want to say, especially in order to insult someone, to show irritation, or to be funny." Oscar Wilde, the great Irish playwright, also known for his biting wit, declared that "sarcasm is the lowest form of wit."

Often we use sarcasm to avoid being direct. Frankly, it is a lazy way to communicate. You are trying to influence behavior, provide a critique, without exercising the courage required to be direct. Stop talking about the things that can go unsaid and exercise the courage to say with clear, direct language the things that need to be said. Saying "don't work too hard" to a worker who is dawdling isn't nearly as helpful as addressing the behavior directly, honestly, and with concern for the success of the worker. Remember, your coaching and corrective feedback must always be aimed at behaviors, not attitudes. Just keep your opinions to yourself.

Tough Love

Iris, a single mom, told us one of the most fantastic stories I've ever heard, and it demonstrates how *dogged determination* is entirely different from *dogmatic declarations*. About four years earlier, as she was cleaning her 15-year-old son's bedroom, she discovered a note that forced her to recognize that he was probably fooling around with drugs at school. When she confronted him, he said, "What do you think you can do about it?"

She didn't make any dogmatic declarations or, as parents too often do, make threats with no intention of following through. Instead, she took him to school, waited outside his class, walked him to the next class, waited outside the class, and walked him to the next class. She kept up this routine for three months. When she shared this story with our class, she said, "Fortunately, I was self-employed."

I would say it was fortunate for her son that she was doggedly determined to apply "tough love" to help him know

171

that she was going to do what she had to do to save him from his addiction, and she was not going to be upset about it.

I wonder what a different world this would be if there were more parents like Iris. What about you? What is your level of commitment? What are you willing to do to handle difficult problems without making dogmatic declarations?

WINNERS SAY:	LOSERS SAY:
I can.	I can't.
I will.	I won't.
I am able.	I'm worried.
I am prosperous.	I'm confused.
I am joyful.	I doubt that.
I am happy.	I don't have enough.
I am in charge.	I can't find it.
I am healthy.	I'm sick.
I am strong.	Nothing can.
I believe.	Nothing will.
I make a decision.	I can't decide.
I remember.	I forgot.
I am thankful.	I tried.
Count on me.	I will never.
I am enthusiastic.	I'm tired.

Actions for Engaging Leaders

- Avoid dogmatic declarations like these:
  "As far as I'm concerned . . ."
  "This is the way it is."
  "That's absurd."
  "That would never work."
  "That's the craziest idea I've ever heard."
  "Where did you get *that* idea?"
  "We've tried that."
  "That would cost too much."

"That would take too much time."
"That's against our policy."
"You have to understand . . ."
"That's impossible."
"That's all there is to it."

- Develop the habit of saying:
"What is your opinion?"
"How do you feel?"
"What do you think?"
"What would you do?"
"Tell me more about that."
"What would the next steps be?"
"It seems to me . . ."
"It appears . . ."
"As far as I can tell . . ."

Benefits You Will Gain

- You'll have a better working relationship with your team.
- Frustration levels will decrease.
- Your team will focus on what's important.
- You'll receive valuable input.

"If I do not believe as you believe, and you do not believe as I believe, all it shows is that I don't believe as you believe and you don't believe as I believe."

Ralph Waldo Emerson

>>>Principle 13

Avoid Arguments

Stu, project manager for a Northwest mechanical contracting company, told us,

I was working at the Hatfield Federal Courthouse for Hanset Stainless, a small architectural metal contractor. I had my first cell phone, a phone so large that it nearly required a backpack to get it around. To refer to this "brick phone" as a mobile device was a partial truth at best!

One of my tasks was procuring and coordinating delivery of material to our job site. The material access to the building was exclusively via tower crane. The tower crane was scheduled in a weekly coordination meeting and time slots were divided into 15-minute increments. We were allowed two slots per week after critical path activities.

During one critical tower crane window, the delivery failed to arrive at the scheduled time. I paced, walked the streets, and repeatedly called the driver, shop, and office, all to no avail. Finally, in a fit of anger and frustration, I threw my cell phone against a column, shattering the phone into a million pieces. Nearly as soon as the phone left my hand, I was approached by a

Hoffman project engineer, who told me that another crane slot was available the following morning. I suddenly realized that my only means for rearranging the missed shipment was shattered all over the slab.

The lesson I learned from this experience is to control my temper. I learned that when I lose my temper, I cut off communication with people, people whose support I need.

Stu's story illustrates in a very dramatic way what often happens as a result of an argument: further communication is hampered. The line of communication and trust that are required for successful project management can never be kept open if we allow the ego to dominate our behavior or break into fits of rage.

If you are one of those who still thinks the only way you can make a point or get the results you need is by hollering and shouting, if you still think that temper tantrums are a sign of manly strength, stop and reexamine some of the costs in broken relationships or the lost respect of your team.

Knowledge is Not Enough

I recently met with the vice president of engineering of a prominent software firm here in the Northwest. This firm employs 400 professional engineers. We discussed the challenges of building a championship team and creating engaged performance at all levels.

"We hire people on the basis of where they went to school, where they have worked, their background, experience, and technical expertise," he told me. "We fire people on the basis of their lack of ability to get along with, relate to, understand, work successfully with, and motivate people."

He went on to say, "Normally, all advancement beyond the entry position is based on the person's ability to work with the team, contribute successfully to the team, and add to the team's success."

Though I have said this many times in many different ways, this manager put it more effectively than I have ever heard it said: "There is a tendency sometimes to think all we need is technical training, and that somehow this education entitles us to the position of responsibility and authority." Knowledge is important, but not enough. Engaging leaders know how to get along with people—how to reach agreements, compromise where needed, gain cooperation and avoid arguments.

Most arguments end with each person more firmly convinced than before that they are absolutely right. You cannot win an argument. If you lose the argument, you have lost. If you win an argument, you lose because you lose a relationship and cause your opponent to feel inferior. You hurt their pride—they will resent you, and you lose the cooperation you wanted—hardly a way to build an engaged team.

Whatever tactics successful leaders adopt in leading people, we find that the best leaders avoid arguments. Their strategy is to use caution in handling opposition and instead influence others by appealing to their interests. Remember: an argument is often harmful and nearly always useless. Induce people to accept your idea without forcing them to admit that they themselves have been in the wrong.

I am not suggesting that you concede important points. When you find it necessary to disagree, do so agreeably: "I understand what you are saying," or "Try to look at it from my point of view for a moment," or "I respect what you are saying, and here may be another way of looking at it," or "I want us to work this out. Let's see if we can find some common ground."

> *"Education is the ability to listen to almost anything without losing your temper or your self-confidence."*
> Robert Frost

Flowers for Not Arguing

Karen, the office manager for a mechanical contractor, told us,

> In May a vendor called to say that we had an invoice from them that was way past due. I confirmed with her that I had the invoice and that it would be paid in two weeks at the 45-day mark. She said, "That's just stupid and a load of bull." I counted to ten and bit my tongue.
>
> I thought her response was a strong overreaction, and it certainly signaled a lack of understanding and professionalism. I told our project manager about the incident. He took the invoice and called their company headquarters in Seattle. Through the process, we found out that they were being bought out by another firm. The new owner's wife called me and apologized for her employee's unprofessional actions. The next day some yellow roses came for me with a note that said, "Sorry about the lady in Seattle. If you need any more help, just let me know."
>
> I could've gotten angry in reaction to the employee's outburst, but instead I kept my cool and continued to answer her questions professionally. As a result, I received both an apology and a bouquet of roses.
>
> The lesson I learned from this experience is that just because someone gets angry with me doesn't mean that I have to lower myself to their level and fight back to prove "they can't do that to me."

I guess we can easily see why the company in Karen's story was selling out. Any time we lose our temper, we are out of control. After all, what does the word "lose" mean? "To become unable to find . . . ," "To have something taken from one . . . ," "To fail to have or get . . . ," "To fail to see, hear, or understand . . . ."[19]

Remember, only those companies who are sharp and on the cutting edge earn the right to remain in the game, stay in business, keep playing for fun and profit. If you cannot control your temper, if you have been one of those people who brags about your temper or uses your ethnic background as an excuse for your temper, now is the time to demonstrate your maturity and leadership by exercising control over your own emotions. You have a responsibility to be an example to all the eyes that look to you as a model of appropriate behavior.

Ranting and Raving

George, paper machine #5 operating assistant for a paper mill in northern Ontario, Canada, told us,

> After several months of onsite help from the Newberg Turbo Paper Group to improve the performance of PM #5, the machine had been running well for several days and the department was much cleaner than I had ever seen it. I entered the control room to greet the machine tender operator and said, "Hi. How are you doing? The machine looks great and is running well. Thanks for a great job."

> He turned to me and went into a rant; "This is all a pile of crap!" On and on he went. Most of his ranting revolved around the enforcement of long-overdue housekeeping standards. I listened, determined not to argue or let him get me upset.

> After he finally finished, I said, "You are a senior experienced operator and you are doing a great job. The younger crew members look up to you. I know change is sometimes hard to accept. With your support of the changes we are making, we can look forward to continuing to run better, which makes everyone's job easier and safer. Please be patient and continue working with the team. The younger guys need your help."

He agreed and thanked me for listening to his rant. After a good day on a clean-running machine, he got to go home feeling good.

The lesson I learned from this experience is when I am confronted with a disgruntled employee, not to react and argue; instead, listen.

Make it easy for members of your team who have a complaint to see you. Let them know that you are eager to listen. Be accessible. By being accessible, you will keep little things from blowing out of proportion. Sometimes the smallest misunderstanding can be blown out of all proportion and, through the rumor mill, will spread like wildfire.

Complaint Restraint

I received the following email from Toby Olsen, sales and marketing manager of the Quality Inn & Suites in Everett, WA. Mr. Olsen was responding to my comments on their customer satisfaction survey. I honestly don't remember what I said. From his response, I must have had some complaint. I do remember and will remember for a long time his generous response.

Hello,

You recently completed a survey in regard to your stay with us. I appreciate your feedback, and I am troubled by the fact that you did not have a perfect stay with us. I appreciate your comments, and I have addressed these with the staff. I hope that you will try us again, and I would like to offer you a special discount on a future stay. Please call me and I will take care of your reservation.

Have a Great Day,
Toby Olsen
Sales & Marketing
Quality Inn & Suites

When I'm back in the Everett area for the evening, I will certainly give his hotel a much higher consideration than any others.

Receiving complaints from dissatisfied customers is part of being in business, part of having customers. There will never be a time when we will not have complaining customers. In spite of this reality, I'm continually amazed at the ineptness of many, if not most, people in their response to complaints.[20]

In *Repeat Business: 6 Steps to Superior Customer Service*, we outline a five-step, pristine process for responding to customer complaints. Arguing with the customer is *not* one of the five steps!

Of course, reading the book doesn't guarantee that when you're pressed and stressed, you will respond with the first of the five steps, a gracious "thank you for bringing the matter to my attention." What I am sure of is this—the more gracious, skillful and capable you and your team are at handling complaints, the more likely you will turn complaining customers into repeat customers who will sing your praises and provide you with referrals.

Turn the Other Cheek

Jim, the safety director for a large Northwest construction company, told us,

> After working with Gene for probably too long, trying to help him do a better job in performing up to our minimum standard, I fired him. A couple of nights later, I walked into a bar not far from our construction site. There sat Gene. I nodded at him. Gene got up, walked over, and spat a big one in my face. I jumped up with my fist cocked. Gene taunted me, "Go ahead and hit me."
>
> The whole scene flashed in front of my eyes. I would hit him in the throat and knock him out or worse. I could see his buddy was ready to pounce on me. I would swing

around before he could get up and knock him flat.

Then I saw the stark fear, the pleading terror in Gene's wife's eyes and thought, "This isn't worth it. What am I trying to prove?" I dropped my fist and said, "Gene, I am sorry for your pain," and walked away. For the first time I can remember, I turned the other cheek."

Controlling our tempers, acting instead of reacting, can take great courage. Sometimes, it appears life does not work out. They said it would be here Tuesday, and it is not. You wanted those contracts signed, and they are not. You were set to go on vacation, and the budget committee tells you there are problems and you are needed at the meetings. People don't show up as scheduled, are late, don't turn reports in on time, leave out important information, skip parts of their job, show up with alcohol on their breath, or worse.

Upsets are a part of our lives. To be empowered, you must learn to move through upsets quickly so they do not interfere with the achievement of your goals. You do not enter into working relationships to become upset.

How do upsets develop? They are usually a result of expectations or agreements not being met, or standards being violated. At the source of many, if not most, unfulfilled expectations is lack of clarity about what exactly was expected by whom, from whom, and by when. What was promised? What was agreed to?

Usually, our first reaction in dealing with upsets is to find fault with the person who did not meet our expectations. We make a silent evaluation of that person's character or competence and avoid interaction to avoid further upset. This can lead to gossip, condemnation, stress, and tension. Consider whose expectation it was in the first place: *yours*. It is therefore *your* responsibility as an engaging leader to see that it is met. The chain of events you can initiate to avoid upsets looks like this:

1. Become crystal clear about the specifics of your expectation.
2. Find someone with whom to entrust the achievement.
3. Clearly communicate the specifics of your expectation.
4. Check to see if the receiver understands the specifics.
5. Ask the receiver to accept responsibility for fulfilling the expectation.
6. Secure a promise to that effect . . . and receive true delivery of the expectation.

There are several links in this communication chain, and when a breakdown occurs, there is always the tendency to blame the other person. The act of blaming eliminates the possibility of correcting the breakdown from your position in the relationship.

If, on the other hand, either party takes 100 percent responsibility to make the situation work and does not hold the other person responsible, the situation can be corrected. When you hold yourself 100 percent responsible, you examine where you did not effectively implement one or more of the links in the communication chain. The question is always "What part did I play in this?" "What can I bring to the interaction now or in the future to make it work?"

Dishes

While it is a simple demonstration, the following anecdote shows how expectations may be conveyed to avoid upsets and arguments:

Cliff asked his daughter to do the dishes. She told him she had done them. He checked the kitchen and found a dishwasher full of dirty dishes, crumbs on the table and counters, and puddles around the sink. His immediate reaction was to do the thing you and I have done too often, which was to allow himself to go out of control, to become upset. After he regained control, he asked his daughter to come to the kitchen for a visit with him. They talked about the standard for cleaning dishes, what that standard looked like, and they entered into what Cliff described as a contract—the contract being that she would not begin watching television until she'd loaded the dishwasher, started it, rinsed the sink, and wiped and dried the table and countertops.

Clarity when delegating or assigning tasks can save so much wasted time, frustration, and, yes, anger, so "clean it up"!

Building Accountability

Dan, superintendent for one of Oregon's top ten general contractors, told us,

> We have had a drywall subcontractor on one of our projects who tended to approach his work in a somewhat disorganized fashion. Early on in the project, he asked me if we could change the sequence of work on the library so that the framing, sheet rock, and associated finish activities could start at the top floor and progress down through the building.
>
> This was the exact opposite from what my original plan was, but I didn't see a problem. In fact, I saw it as an opportunity to engage him in a more thoughtful, better-organized approach to his work. The change would be his idea, and I have been learning there is no better way to motivate and hold people positively accountable than to let it be their idea.
>
> The other key subs on the project found this proposal acceptable, so the schedule was changed to reflect the drywall subcontractor's request. I was excited because it looked like we had found the answer to helping him better organize his part of the project, which was important to all the other people involved.
>
> One day while walking the building, I noticed that the third floor had been completely finished. The second floor was in various states of completion with some

framing missing. To my disappointment and dismay, I saw most of the drywall completed; however, several areas had not been taped, the ceiling grid was left 50 percent complete, and no one was working on this floor. I went on down to the first floor, where the drywall sub's entire crew was hard at work.

Keeping Turbo's 5-step DARE+ Correction Process[21] in mind, the next day after our daily coordination meeting, I pulled the drywall foreman aside and reminded him that the finish sequence had been changed at his request to start at the top floor and work our way down. Then I said, "I saw that your entire crew was on the first floor when the second floor was not yet completed" and asked him what happened.

He had no explanation. I told him that when he approaches his work haphazardly, it is difficult for the rest of the subcontractors to follow him. This costs the other subs time and money in lost productivity.

After a few minutes of discussion, he agreed and committed to having the second floor completely taped and ready for paint within two days. I thanked him for his cooperation and commitment to the success of the project.

"The lesson I learned from this experience is that the 5-step correction process is a far more effect way to handle broken promises and unmet agreements than my old approach of getting mad and losing my temper.

Confrontation is not easy. Remember the person you are confronting is as human as you are. As Lillian Glass, author of *Say It . . . Right: How to Talk in Any Social or Business Situation*, says, "The key is respect. Yes, you're hurt. But after you've let out your point of view, you have to allow the other person the dignity to find a solution and make it work. You can't be a perfect judge of another person or a particular situation because you don't know the nuances that go into it."

Confrontation is not a competition. Whatever competing you do on company time should be with yourself.

Withholding

Frequently, people hold back communication about what is not working well out of a desire to be liked or to avoid the possibility of rejection—in other words, to preserve the relationship. Closer examination reveals that withholding upsets or kills a relationship. Without communication, there is no relationship.

When you hold back your negative disappointment about unmet agreements or broken promises, you carry them around and view the person you have withheld them from through a special pair of glasses tinted by your judgments. "I can't ask Leo to do this; he never gets anything back on time." Soon, we discover we have less and less to say to the person we have withheld from, and we ultimately write the person off as a non-contributor. Now there is even more hopelessness about the situation.

The cost of withholding communication about upsets is your relationship with people. Put yourself in the position of the one no one is talking to. When you "have egg on your face," do you want people to think those nasty things we think about people with egg on their faces? Or worse yet, do you want them to talk to each other about that egg on your face? When a team is committed to each member, and each member to the whole, in true partnership, people are willing to say and listen to anything about one another.

Two tools for handling upsets are *coaching* and *correction*. Coaching is feedback regarding the unsuccessful fulfillment of expectations when the person did not know how to fulfill the expectation. It is given with the intention of teaching people whatever it is they are not yet fully able to execute to the desired standard. Correction is feedback regarding the unsuccessful fulfillment of understood and agreed-upon standards and expectations. Correction is required when people fail to perform up to their previously demonstrated capability.

Project Barriers

Tim, operations manager for a major Northwest paving company, told us,

I was managing a project on I-405 near Bothell, WA. We were widening several bridges and adding a lane in both directions on a three-mile stretch of the interstate. The contract had numerous design issues and changes, and was soon way behind schedule. If things weren't resolved, the project would take an additional 12 months.

After exhaustive negotiations, we arrived at a plan with WDOT to re-sequence the project in an attempt to get things back on track and successfully meet the new completion schedule. We would compress the schedule and have multiple parts of the project happening simultaneously rather than the linear fashion of the initial schedule. The traffic alignment had to be repositioned to get the project going again. One key piece of work remained to accomplish this—constructing a short segment of concrete barriers.

The barrier work was to be constructed by a subcontractor who would position the concrete barrier with a slip-form paving machine. We had constructed the foundation, built access, tied the reinforcing steel, and made everything ready for this subcontractor. We had engaged them in the work flow change process and reached an agreement on their added costs and a schedule for them to perform their work. This would open the way for getting the project back on track. We were all set to go.

On the morning that the barrier subcontractor was to begin the work, I met their superintendent on the job site.

I vividly recall meeting him at the end of the off-ramp. He drove up in his rattletrap purple Ford Ranger pickup. He told me they had a change in schedule and would not be starting that day. He told me he would have to get back to me on when they might be available to begin.

I was fuming mad. I reminded him that we had met with both the agency and his company, negotiated the changes and extra costs, and that his company owner had committed to performing the work necessary to help get the project back on track.

No matter, he wasn't going to have anyone working that day. I lost all control and sense of reason and proceeded to dress him up one side and down the other. I called him every name in the book. I saw red! While I was exploding and screaming at him, he just got in his truck and drove off.

The lesson I learned from this experience is that losing my temper and yelling and screaming is rarely, if ever, the answer. After a brief conversation with his superiors, the situation was resolved, their work was completed, and the project moved forward.

"Between stimulus and response there is a space.
In that space is our power to choose our response.
In our response lies our growth and freedom."
                                        Victor Frankl

Ensuring Accountability

Tim was supervising an important construction project. The drywall firm that had won the contract with its low bid was not performing well. There were several days when the crew didn't even show up. Tim reported this to the office.

I was carefully documenting all these workers' no-shows and other examples of poor performance. They were officially notified that if they did not start performing as agreed, they would be replaced. As it turned out, this crew didn't seem to take our notice seriously and chose not to pick up their performance. Since all legal steps had been taken, we were ready to let them go.

In the meantime, I had secured another drywall company, and that team was already on standby. We asked the original drywall firm to leave per our formal notification process. We gave the crew ample time and appropriate notice.

Amazingly, the standby company came in and completed the job in three days—the same job the other company has already wasted *three weeks* NOT doing!

The lesson I learned from this experience is to not argue or complain or play the victim, saying, "There's nothing I can do," when a crew refuses to take accountability for its own work. I learned instead to proactively and productively work to solve problems. I may not like all of the laws that comprise the playing field, but complaining about what I can't control, change, or affect just robs me of my power. I get power when I take the kind of constructive action that gets results. In this case, the solution to the problem was documenting everything and having a good backup plan in place.

It may be difficult to find people who have the self-discipline to adhere to high standards without outside coaching, direction, and, yes, discipline. The leader who resorts to arguing, harassment, sarcasm, attacking, or ignoring poor performance is derelict in their responsibility and will never earn respect or get the results required to create an engaged, high-performance team.

Expect the best of others. If and when the people in your world fall below your agreed-upon standard of excellence and commitment, document early and accurately. Communication, documentation, and preparation will usually prompt people to be accountable. When separation is required, you can take that step with confidence, and your projects will come in ahead of schedule. You will maintain your own sense of healthy power and self-esteem.

Actions for Engaging Leaders

- Listen silently to ideas you do not agree with.
- Constructively hold team members accountable to standards.
- Be proactive in the enforcement of your company's performance standards
- Count to ten before you respond.

Benefits You Will Gain

- Difficult situations will be easier to handle.
- Your team will emulate your professional style.
- You will gain self-confidence as you deal with disciplinary issues.
- You will be seen as a competent, professional leader.

"Get your adversary saying 'Yes, yes,' immediately!"
Socrates

>>>Principle 14

Begin With Yes, Yes

Although it was over 30 years ago, I'll never forget—we had just finished our weekly company meeting. As usual, I'd been actively engaged in sharing many of my opinions, some of which, I suppose, were decidedly different from other people's. Ralph, president of our company, said, "Larry, do you have a 'rule-of-the-week card' in your pocket?" It was a pretty good bet that I did.

At that time, I taught a 12-week sales course at least twice each week. At the end of each session, every class member, including myself, signed a "rule-of-the-week card" and took the pledge to apply that week's sales skill for the following week and prepare to report on its use at the next session.

I reached into my pocket and handed my card to Ralph. He wrote on it in large letters, "CUSHION."

I certainly knew what "CUSHION" meant: I taught an extraordinary session on the need for, value of, and use of cushions in selling situations. The idea is to "never disagree with the prospect about anything until you first agree with them about something." I taught the session with conviction and was consciously practicing this skill in selling situations.

Ralph said, "You know, the principle of cushioning

responses applies in more than selling situations. Why don't you try using cushions in your conversations here in the office for a week?" As I thought about some of my interactions in our company meeting, I knew Ralph was right; I could be more gracious, more professional, more agreeable, and probably get better results if I practiced using cushions.

This is how a cushion works in a selling situation: The prospect says, "I want to think about it." The cushion: "I know you want make the right decision." The prospect says, "The price is too high." The cushion: "This is an important investment." The prospect says, "I don't think I'd be able to figure out how to use it." The cushion: "When I first started learning how to use it, I was pretty unsure of myself too." You get the idea.

So a great practice in all interactions is begin with "yes, yes." In other words, begin by getting in step. When you are endeavoring to sell an idea and encounter resistance, your first response isn't

- "I don't care what you think."
- "I don't agree; you're wrong again."
- "I don't think you know what you're talking about."
- "I've got a better idea."

Instead of starting with these disagreeable disagreements, preface your response with some simple point of agreement. Why should it ever be necessary to say, "I don't agree with you"? Can't you say, "That's an interesting way to look at it" or "I hadn't thought about it that way"?

Instead of saying, "That will never work," why not say in neutral tones, "I know we both want a successful outcome. Tell me more about how you see it working."

These questions, asked sincerely and in neutral tones, can all be simple, effective ways to cushion your first response.

So I used Ralph's handcrafted "rule-of-the-week card" for many weeks and, although I still catch myself from time to time forgetting to take a moment before I respond (or should I say react—those times when ego rules), I more often than not find it easy to begin with a cushion. This takes a lot of the stress out of life and relationships. So how would you like to reduce stress and tension, and increase the ease of getting your ideas accepted? *Begin with yes, yes,* and you'll be more effective.

Now let's turn to how engaging leaders use "yes, yes" when presenting ideas.

Someone said long ago that "the first ten words of your presentation are more important than the next ten thousand." Perhaps an exaggeration, but the point is well made. Begin your presentation in a way that overcomes inertia, breaks through some natural resistance by helping the other person focus on mutually-desired end results. Get their physical as well as psychological head nodding, and you may have won half the battle.

We must remember that everyone, with the exception of a few saints, operate out of self-interest—we are all listening to the same radio station, WIFM—**W**hat's **I**n it **F**or **M**e? To think otherwise is to fail to recognize the fundamentals of human nature and human motivation. When moving things forward or changing direction, you must expect to meet with opposing points of view, different agendas, vested interests, fear, and the natural resistance to change.

So how do you do this? It may be as simple as stopping for a moment before you present your ideas and asking yourself, "What do we both want here?"

- We want the project to be a success.
- We want to ensure safety.
- We want what's best for the customer.
- We want to preserve the dignity of our employees.

- We'd like to be known as an industry leader.
- We always want to be seen as fair, honest, and caring.

The idea you have in mind must have one or more of these advantages. If there are no benefits to all concerned, perhaps you should go back to the drawing board and ask yourself, "What are the benefits of my proposal beyond what I want, beyond me getting what I need?" This effort isn't always easy because we're so wrapped up in our own self-interest, our own "what's in it for me?" As you think about your proposal, apply Leadership Principle #5: See Their Point of View. Find some special advantage, some special benefit that you both want.

This is how you begin your presentation—"I know we both want this project to be safe," "I know we are all eager to see how we can reduce costs to bring this project back under budget," "I have an idea that I believe could help us reduce costs, speed up our progress, make our project safer, make our customers happier, or earn us all a bonus."

You might start by saying, "I've been thinking about what you said last week in our staff meeting; how important it is to you that we work together more as a team, and I have an idea that could contribute to our successful teamwork." As you employ the earlier Leadership Principles—Lead from High Ideals, Become Genuinely Interested, Don't Criticize, Condemn, or Complain, See Their Point of View, Be an Active Listener—you will find it easy to form your message in a way that begins by getting a "yes, yes."

Emphasize that your only difference may be one of method, not of purpose. When people are saying "Yes," they are moving forward, accepting, with an open attitude. The more "Yesses" you can get, the more likely you are to succeed in securing their cooperation and support for your ultimate proposal. When they are saying "Yes," they are listening. When you get a "No," they are thinking about why they are right.

Negotiation

Make a point of considering in advance the resistance you may encounter. Consider others' objections as wants and needs that may interfere with your proposal. Take those wants and needs into account when you make your presentation plans. If possible, modify your proposal to satisfy their needs. When you encounter objections or resistance of any kind, ask yourself, "Can this point be conceded without risking my main purpose?" When you are bringing people around to your way of thinking, make as many minor concessions as you can.

If you are up against strong resistance to your main point, you might be wise to delay the issue. This gives the other person a chance to reconsider and provides you with an opportunity to reorganize your campaign. Under ordinary conditions, advance your ideas in a modest way that invites agreement, not in the pushy manner that provokes opposition.

The Winning Number

Mark, general manager for a local mechanical contracting company, told us,

> When we were asked us to pick a new 5X (five times more) enthusiasm goal, I chose getting business from new clients.
>
> I had a very large project that I was preparing a proposal for. Several general contractors we had never quoted were bidding this project. What I decided to do was apply five times more enthusiasm on reaching out to contact all of these generals.
>
> I decided to work hard with each of the estimators individually to get to know them and what each of them required in our proposal. In order to have each of these contractors allow me into their company "inner circles," I needed to apply several of Turbo's Leadership Principles: #1, Lead from High Ideals; #14, Begin with Yes, Yes; and #6, Be an Active Listener. They all had a

little different twist, so our proposal went out several different ways.

My approach was 100 percent successful and, in the end, the top three bidders all used my proposal in the preparation of their respective bids. We will be doing work on this project!

It's easy for us to settle into routines that are almost monotonous, even in the priority areas of our lives. In the story above, Mark tried something different and got the contract he wanted. Have you been told selling is a numbers game? Selling is more much more than a numbers game. After you identify priority prospects, find a way to *Begin with a Yes, Yes.* Apply the passion of renewed commitment—and all the statistics will change in your favor.

It's Your Move

At times, you'll think you've got nothing in common with someone you must sell your ideas to. Alex, staff accountant for a local firm, was surprised to find common interests with someone he considered his enemy. He told us,

My relationship with my boss was static, stoic, tense, and fearful. Whenever she and I interacted, it was almost always on the basis of correcting me for a mistake I had made. I became resistant to her and was reluctant to initiate much of anything when she was in my presence. At times, I secretly wished that she would not come within the vicinity of my desk. I became judgmental of her and considered her my enemy.

One day not long after I had selected her as my "pearl" (someone with whom you want to improve your relationship), she asked me out to lunch. I was totally shocked! At lunch we had a great conversation about our workplace and, to my amazement, we actually agreed on many topics! "Begin with Yes, Yes"—with an emphasis on where both parties are in agreement—was in full effect. I was amazed to discover that she is a dynamic individual and that we have a lot of beliefs in common.

From Doubtful to Trusting

Michelle, controller for a local construction company, told us,

Yesterday our contracts administrator came into my office to tell me how the training is going with Jenny, our administrative receptionist. She seemed concerned about Jenny being able to cover for her while she is out on maternity leave. She was worried that Jenny will become overwhelmed and shut down, throw in the towel and just let things pile up.

After listening for a few minutes, I said, "I understand your concern. We should remember that there are always two sides to these kinds of issues." Jenny had been in my office the day before, talking about her frustrations and concerns. I continued, "You know what you are doing. You are an extremely talented woman. What about looking at this situation as a challenge rather than a chore?" Then I asked her if we could try some of the techniques we've been learning in the Leadership Development Lab. She said, "Yes, let's give it a try." That was the "yes" I was looking for.

We started out with a blank piece of paper and soon came up with an outlined list of the training she wanted to accomplish the next day. We thoroughly discussed the training she wanted to complete and printed it out so both she and Jenny could have their training objectives in front of them at the beginning of each day. Then I went to our whiteboard and wrote down Turbo's 3-Step On-the-Job Training Process—tell and show; tell as they do; ask them to tell as they do.[22] She agreed that she would use the process the next morning.

When I got back to our office from a meeting that day and was getting a cup of coffee I noticed that there was a piece of paper they were both looking at, and it had a few lines crossed out. I realized they were working with the 3-Step On-the-Job Training Process. Woo-hoo! It was so cool to see them getting along and actually smiling and talking about what Jenny needed to learn and do to get fully up to speed.

The lesson I learned from this experience is to listen, really listen—listen to more than the words; listen to the emotional content, the feeling and fears behind the words—so I can shape my message in a way that gets a "yes, yes" response.

Partnering

A few years ago, I conducted an introductory session to Construction Partnering for the Associated General Contractors in Seattle, WA. A couple hundred contractors filled the room, and more kept filing in, one after another. These contractors had shown up to see if there really was an alternative to litigation, the ultimate conclusion of unresolved disagreements. One of the senior contractors in the room came up to me and said, "I've been a general contractor for 36 years. I've spent more money on legal fees in the past three years than in the first 33 years combined. There must be a better way."

Isn't it time for us to find ways to disagree in agreeable ways, to end disputes before they're out of control? There are ways to resolve upsets and to avoid them. Make it a habit to *begin with yes, yes.*

Shirts

David, the president of a major Willamette Valley professional landscape company, applied this principle when he had to confront one of his foremen. He told us,

It was midmorning when I showed up at one of our job sites in West Linn. Gary, the foreman, and his crew were already quite busy on the project. It was a beautiful, sunny summer morning. I could tell it was going to be a hot one. After I had finished setting up the crew with a few changes and some special customer requests, I jumped in my pickup truck and drove off.

Then I remembered I hadn't posted one of our promotional "Landscaping by . . ." yard signs at the job site. When I returned to the site, only 20 to 30 minutes later, the crew had already taken off their company uniform shirts. This is a direct policy violation, and they knew it. Our company shirts are made of soft, lightweight fabric specially designed to breathe well. They are loose around the neck to help the workers stay cool on hot summer days.

When the crew saw my pickup heading their way, the shirts went back on immediately and the crew scattered. When I approached Gary, he knew what was coming.

Rather than point out the obvious policy violation, I tried a more constructive approach. I decided to begin by *getting in step*. I complimented Gary on the crew's progress and the quality of the landscape job they had already completed that morning. I acknowledged Gary for his 15 successful years with the company and pointed out how the crew looks up to him as an example. Then I reminded him of the reason of the shirt policy— they make our crew and our company look professional. I pointed out that the shirts were selected because they add to the client's sense of security, build the team's esprit de corps, and especially because they are comfortable to wear even on hot August days.

Gary seemed to accept what I said about the importance of wearing the uniforms and showed respect for my request that the uniform shirt policy be followed. We haven't had a problem with engagement with the standard since.

The lesson I learned is it pays to be positive and *begin with yes, yes*. I need to always get in step with my team and point out their strengths even when my first response might be to let them have it.

One last word: if your agenda is to get the upper hand, to prove the other person wrong, to prove how smart you are, how right you are, how clever you are—if you care more about how you look than what is right and best—you may never be successful with this simple *Begin with Yes, Yes* leadership principle. It must be clear that your only desire is that the best result—safety, productivity, process improvement, high morale, happy customers, ease, and fairness—is achieved. You must be seen as sincerely desiring a win-win outcome.

Actions for Engaging Leaders

- Begin by discussing the points on which you agree.
- Consider in advance the objections you may encounter.
- Be willing to compromise on minor points.
- Make your standards a win-win-win; a win for your customer, a win for your employees, a win for your company.

Benefits You Will Gain

- You will gain the cooperation of your team.
- Your team will present a consistent, unified front.
- You will look good to your customers and the public.
- You will reduce turnover and retain customers.

"Noble be man, helpful and good!
For that alone sets him apart from
every other creature on earth."
Goethe

>>>Principle 15

Appeal to Their Noble Motives

Todd shared a lesson he learned about the human desire to have integrity:

I was leadman for the finishing work on a commercial remodel project, for which we were being paid on an hourly basis. I was training Fred, a friend, in finish carpentry. Fred told me he wanted to work extra hours, starting his day at three o'clock in the morning. There was a lot of work in front of us, so I agreed to let him start before I got to the job.

After a few days, it became apparent that Fred was not accomplishing much in those early hours. When I confronted Fred about his lack of productivity, he admitted to lying about his hours. He hadn't been coming in early and putting in the extra hours he was charging me for. He said his lie was eating at him and he was feeling pretty miserable about it. We resolved the situation by working out a payback plan.

The lesson learned from this experience is that people feel better when they are honest and have integrity in all things.

Everyone likes to think of themselves as honest, fair, and reliable—we want others to see us as someone who can be counted on. Having integrity gives us a sense of inner peace. Todd's friend wanted to be able to think well of himself, but didn't have the strength of will to live up to his own standards. He experienced relief and renewed joy in his work when Todd helped him live up to the noble motive of honesty and integrity. In order to lead people, appeal to their noble motives: "You know the right thing to do!" "I can always trust you." "The team is counting on you." "You never let us down." "I appreciate your honesty and integrity." "These are the values of our company. Do you feel in harmony with them? Can we count on you to live up to these high ideals?"

Most companies have a published mission and vision statement, and often a list of stated values. If yours doesn't, you can create a list for your department, your area of responsibility. You can develop your own personal mission and vision and your own set of personal values. Ask yourself, "What do I stand for?" When you can point to your values, the values of your department, it becomes easier for you to appeal to the noble motives of those who work with you. You simply ask them to live up to the values that you are expecting of them, live up to the values they agreed to when they signed on. Tell them that you know they have every intention of living up to the company's high standards. Show them how the actions you're asking for will help them live up to, support, and model your stated values. Create engagement by appealing to your team's noble motives.

Missing Tools

Dale appealed to the noble motives of an angry crew member. He told us,

> During a period of explosive growth in our shop, I asked Bob to help out in a production area. He agreed. Then midafternoon, I discovered Bob walking off the

job because someone had "stolen" one of his tools. He said he wouldn't work with someone petty enough to steal. I told Bob we really needed his help and if his square didn't turn up, I would buy him a new one. I asked him to put himself above this petty thief and to please return to the job. The next day Bob came to me and apologized.

The lesson I learned was the importance of confronting difficult and challenging behaviors. At first I was afraid to confront Bob, but by appealing to his noble motives, he became willing to pitch in and overcome his childish anger.

Four Inches Short

I was impressed when Steven told us the following story, which demonstrates the importance of appealing to noble motives when asking someone to redo their work, even when it seems like cutting corners on excellence wouldn't hurt anyone:

> We were installing all the electrical systems for three buildings, including the piping for the security system contractor. I assigned Chuck to install all the conduit stubs for security sensors on 17 large power garage doors. After walking the jobsite and reviewing the prints and layouts with Chuck, I left him to make the installation.

> Since most of the doors were alike, Chuck decided he could save time by pre-cutting and bending the conduit. The next afternoon as I made my rounds, Chuck was nearing completion, except that on about every third door, the conduit was four inches short. When I asked what happened, he said he'd made a mistake with his measurements but was going to cut four-inch pieces and then strap them on.

> We walked the job, looking at the rest of the work. I complimented Chuck on his work and told him how

professional the job looked. Then I told him that although the four-inch pieces would work, it wouldn't look as professional as the rest of his work. I asked him if he would go ahead and take all the short conduits down and re-cut new ones to the proper length.

After he had made the changes and the job was officially complete, I could see how proud he was of his work.

The lesson I learned from this experience is the importance of calling my team to the noble motives of craftsmanship and professionalism. I learned that when I appeal to these noble motives, my team gets to correct their mistakes and take great pride in their work.

H. Jackson Brown expressed the value of high personal standards—noble motives—in a powerful way: "Good character is more to be praised than outstanding talent. Most talents are, to some extent, a gift. Good character, by contrast, is not given to us. We have to build it piece by piece—by thought, choice, courage, and determination." [23]

Lights Out

Roger, warehouse distribution center manager for an electrical wholesaler, told us,

Two Fridays ago, we suddenly lost power at the warehouse. A storm front had blown in, and a large gust of wind snapped a nearby power pole like a twig. When the pole came down, the transformer blew up. Dangerous high voltage lines lay across the street and blocked the entrance to our parking lot. We found ourselves in the dark, cut off from the world, with only cell phones and a lot of incomplete work. No one could get into or out of our warehouse.

There was a lot of pressure to continue operating in the distribution center. There was a little illumination from the overhead sky lights. I didn't feel it would be safe enough and refused to take any chances of someone getting hurt. The swing shift team leader called to say that, due to the street closures, he was unable to find a way to get to work. I told him we needed him and to keep trying. Finally, after much frustration, he arrived hours late. He was extremely perturbed and about to turn around and go back home.

I applied the same leadership principle I followed when I insisted that our employees not drive the fork lift equipment in the dark. I appealed to his noble motives by reminding him of the hundreds of coworkers and thousands of customers who were counting on him to achieve his mission.

He asked me how that was possible. I asked him if he had any ideas. He said there were miner-style flashlights in inventory that they could use while pulling hand carts around to fill orders. I put Leadership Principle #8, "Validate Their Ideas," to use. It seemed to be the only option anyway, short of giving up and going home.

He and his crew actually had fun that night. The power didn't come back on until their shift was almost over, yet they successfully filled and shipped every order.

In the past when this kind of thing occurred, it would take us weeks to catch up. Since the swing shift team completed their normal work load, we avoided getting behind and this was, by far, the fastest recovery we have ever experienced from a major interruption.

The lesson I learned from this experience is that when I "appeal to noble motives" and let solutions be "their idea," I get full engagement. Each of us have deeply rooted values that guide our motives and actions. When I can tap into the nobility of others, the results exceed my highest expectations.

Brother's Keeper

Amity, bookkeeper for a fruit marketing company in Yakima, WA, told us,

About 14 years ago, when my husband Todd and I first got married, it seemed like everyone in the family got along great. We were like a wonderful, lustrous pink pearl, at least on the surface. Everything was smooth and shiny, but underneath, there was the continual irritation of old hurts, misunderstandings, and childish jealousy. This was keeping us from having the rich, intimate relationships we all want with family and friends.

As time went by, there were fewer and fewer family gatherings. When we did get together, there were absentees who always had lots of excuses. Our shallow conversations only skimmed the surface, mostly about sports and, of course, our kids. There always seemed to be a hard-to-describe tension in the air, the proverbial "walking on egg shells."

Two years ago, my mother-in-law told me how much the discord was hurting her. It was her plea for me to do something. Little did I know, she had also told my sister-in-law. Sometime later, my sister-in-law called me to talk about what was going on. I decided to take the opportunity to hash it out. I started by asking my husband about what was going on between him and his brother from his perspective. We decided to leave all the angst in the past and start fresh, giving each family member the benefit of the doubt.

Over the next six months, we gradually rebuilt our family's relationships. Gatherings were more frequent and a lot more fun. I am so thankful that I acted on the opportunity to help repair the relationships because this last year, my husband's brother was taken from us suddenly. Instead of regret, I have peace of mind knowing that I had a part in the brothers regaining the harmony they both wanted.

The lesson I learned from this experience is that when opportunities arise to help solve problems in relationships that matter, I need to act, seize the initiative, and not let fear hold me back.

Sometimes people need someone to appeal to the values they have strayed from—in this case, the noble motives of harmony and grace.

> *"The golden moments in the stream of life rush past us and we see nothing but sand; the angels come to visit us, and we only know them when they are gone."*
>
> George Elliott

Follow the Leader

Richard, manager for a restaurant chain in Yakima, WA, discovered that living with courage and high ideals is the best way to appeal to the noble motives of others:

When I was a junior at Lincoln High School in Tacoma, WA, I wasn't sure what I wanted to do next with my life. I thought about the Air Force and even took a tour of Fort Lewis and McChord in Washington. Another idea was to go to college. This was a pretty radical, out-of-the-box idea for me. No one in my immediate or extended family had gone to college. In fact, my older brother followed my father's example and didn't get past the ninth grade.

My high school had just been approved for the Bill Gate's Achievers program, which provides scholarships for high school graduates who would otherwise not be able to go to college due to their family's financial disadvantages. My grades and high school achievements, along with our family's status, made me eligible.

I nervously took the first step by applying. I was surprised and excited when I learned that I was approved for the scholarship. That summer I checked out several colleges and found a school I loved—Central Washington University. The second step in my plan was complete. I applied and was very excited the day I found out that I had been accepted. The third step was now complete.

After my freshman year at CWU, something happened that I certainly never would have expected— my mom decided to go back to school to get her massage therapist license. That same year, my sister who had had a baby at 16 started attending Clover Park Technical College. My third year in college, my youngest sister graduated from high school. The next year, I graduated from college with a BS in nutrition and food service management, my sister graduated from Clover Park with her associates degree, and my younger sister started school for massage therapy and finished with her license shortly after.

The lesson I learned from my experience is that my actions affect the decisions others make. Even when I don't realize it, others are watching me and making decisions that will affect the rest of their lives. I had a greater influence and impact on their choices than I could have imagined.

A Family Affair

Steve, senior project manager for a local mechanical contractor, told us,

I was in my second year of a four-year pipe fitting apprenticeship with Local Union #695 Plumbers and Pipefitters of Longview/Kelso, WA. Due to the failing economy, work in our local jurisdiction had come to a screeching halt. Most of the journeymen in our local had taken out "travel cards" and were being dispatched to projects across the Northwest. As apprentices, we were not eligible to travel. We continued attending our apprenticeship classes at night and spent our days doing odd jobs to pay the bills. We would stop in at the union hall in hopes that a call would come in from a small local project needing apprentices.

One morning at breakfast I came across a newspaper article about a non-profit organization called Community Home Health and Hospice, which provided comfort care for patients diagnosed with terminal illnesses. The organization was planning to build a facility in Longview and was reaching out to the community in search of volunteers with construction experience.

A few of the other apprentices and I talked about it. We approached one of our instructors, a licensed plumber, to see if he would lead us in a volunteer effort to perform the plumbing scope for the project. Over the course of the next four to five weeks we worked 40 hours a week and successfully completed the project, passing all of the system testing and required inspections. That fall, Longview's Community Home Health and Hospice Center opened its doors and began accepting patients.

I gained an overwhelming sense of pride in knowing that I could use the skills of my chosen profession to help others. The greatest sense of achievement came seven years later in 1988. The Longview Hospice facility completed a small expansion project and invited community volunteers to help plant flowers in preparation for an open house. My wife and I decided to take our two sons, ages five and four. We spent the day digging and planting in the garden areas surrounding the facility. It was an amazing feeling to show our children the facility I had helped build and instill in them the importance of operating from the noble motive of helping others in need, the joy of giving back to our community.

As our three sons continued to grow, we kept alert for opportunities in our community to help out—building homes for Habitat for Humanity, delivering meals for Meals on Wheels, and collecting and distributing canned foods for the Community Action Program. The most rewarding thing for me is seeing our adult children operate from noble motives as they continue involvement in their communities. I know when they have children, they will pass on the great experiences and opportunities of giving back.

Operating from noble motives—and, by example, teaching our children to do the same—is good for our culture. It helps create the kinds of communities we want to live in.

Forklift Leadership

Earlier this summer, Don stopped by our office. It had been over twelve years since I had seen him. He had been a very engaged participant in one of our Klamath Falls Leadership Development Labs. When he retired, his heart called him to New Orleans, where he worked on the construction of Habitat for Humanity homes to help with the recovery after Hurricane Katrina. There he fell in love and married and moved with his wife to Metairie, Louisiana, where she grew up. Don was back in Oregon to see his family when he stopped by our place after taking his Dad out to McMinnville to see the "Spruce Goose."

When Don became eligible for retirement, his employer's vice president of human resources made a special trip all the way from Portland down to southern Oregon just to see him. She wanted him to know that he was more than welcome to stay on; he really didn't have to retire until he was 72.

Early in Don's career he was a "log peeler." He became an expert in the art of peeling logs for the veneers used in plywood manufacturing. When the plywood mill closed, Don went to work in his company's neighboring particleboard plant. When Don joined the LDL, he was working on the night shift crew. At that time, they were producing about 2500 pieces of particleboard per shift. Over time, with innovation and motivation, the night shift got their production up to 8000 pieces per shift! This is over three times more output, a huge improvement.

Even with these increases in production, the company faced extreme competitive pressures. It became more and more apparent that they had to further reduce their labor costs if they were going to remain competitive and keep running. Over 25 percent of the particleboard mills in America were closed and permanently shuttered in the 90s due to recessions and the substitution of new products for particleboard.

To further reduce the plants' operating costs, they eliminated the cleanup positions. The cleanup's job was to sweep out underneath the particleboard production line where the chips and sawdust fall.

Don operated a forklift, transferring loads from the press to the sander. He took the initiative to get down off his forklift several times during his shift to sweep things up and clean things out so quality wouldn't suffer and productivity wouldn't slow down. Don was on the receiving end of a lot of chiding from some of the crew for going the extra mile, doing more than his job description called for. This didn't stop him; he kept right on doing the extra work. He took great pride in his contribution to his shift's extraordinary production.

After a while, others on his shift began to join him in the cleanup effort instead of complaining about the company laying off the clean-up guys. Don didn't let the crew intimidate him into doing as little as he could get away with. Instead he led them to take pride in going the extra mile. His team brought discretionary effort to the job, continued to set production records, and the mill continues to run successfully.

Don, through his example, appealed to his crew's noble motives of pride and teamwork to overcome cynicism and negative peer pressure, and to give a little more discretionary effort.

Count to Ten

Sheila, controller for a Clark County construction company, told us,

> When we were challenged to improve an important relationship, I chose one of my coworkers. She started working for our company six years ago. She was originally hired as the receptionist and accounts payable assistant and has been promoted to contracts administrator. She is an important asset to our company. We can count on her projects being accurate and complete as long as they are in her "normal realm." She takes great pride in her work, but change is not a thing she handles well. In fact, if anyone makes a change or asks her to do something out of her normal procedures, you risk her wrath. She has become an extremely negative person. She spends a lot of time complaining. She seems to feel better about herself when pointing out the mistakes other people make.
>
> At a recent administrative meeting, I asked everyone to focus on a module of our upgraded accounting software that tracks and integrates. I asked her to test it and see if it could help our team function at a higher level. She was immediately on the defensive, crossing her arms and giving us dirty looks. I focused on the positive: her work is always fabulous. I asked her to see if this new module would help us be more flexible as we grow, help us with tracking, and give us the tools we needed for greater speed and accuracy.
>
> The meeting was a very long 30 minutes with as much brainstorming as possible. She was negative throughout most of the meeting, but in the last 10

minutes, she finally started to see that it could work, as long as she didn't have to go back and redo what she had already completed this year. This was a start.

Then this last week, out of the blue she mentioned the new quote-tracking system and how it would benefit us. I was surprised and pleased that she was trying to do what is best for the team.

The lesson I learned from this experience is that patience and appealing to noble motives of efficiency and teamwork ensures acceptance of new ideas and can improve my relationships.

The Price of Success

What is the price of success? The price of success is consistently adhering to your personal standards and ideals, no matter how tempting it is at times to compromise, take short cuts, and just slide by.

Success means that you must have a high and sustained determination to put into action what you plan to accomplish, not just when circumstances are favorable to its accomplishment, but in spite of all adverse circumstances that may arise. Nothing worthwhile has ever been accomplished without some obstacles to overcome.

Success means refusing to believe that there are any circumstances sufficiently strong to defeat you in the accomplishment of your purpose, and it means paying the price of seeing your standards and ideals being challenged.

Hard? I should say so! That's why many people never attempt to consistently live up to noble motives. They answer the siren call of the rut and remain on the beaten paths of the masses. Everything worthwhile has been achieved with constant endeavor, a measure of pain, and the persistence of ambition.

Everyone must ask, "Am I willing to endure the pain of this struggle for the comforts, rewards, and glory that go with achievement? Or shall I accept the uneasy contentment of mediocrity? Am I willing to pay the price of success?" Know the pride and power of lived purposes.

Actions for Engaging Leaders

- When a situation arises that lends itself to dishonesty, use that situation to prove your honesty and integrity.
- Call your team to the higher ground inspired by noble motives.
- Act in ways that inspire others to act on their noble motives.
- Seek opportunities to generously give back to your community.
- Confront situations with difficult people by appealing to their noble motives.

Benefits You Will Gain

- You'll gain a quality reputation.
- You will gain an inner joy and satisfaction because your example moved someone to make a positive change in their life.
- You will establish a value system to be passed on from generation to generation.
- You will have the power of purpose.
- You may be astonished with the success your team enjoys.

>>>Part Three

Continuous Improvement

"Leaders who get their team members to solve their own problems are making a sound investment that will pay off with many benefits: their team members will become less dependent on them, more self-directing, more self-sufficient, and more capable of solving problems on their own."

Thomas Gordon

Practical Problem Solving

What is a problem? A problem is that which stands between you and steady progress toward your goals: continuous improvement in quality, customer service, market penetration, product improvements, profit, and fun.

Excellent companies recognize that every problem represents an opportunity for learning and improvement. Complacency about problem solving, especially the practice of transferring blame to customers, suppliers, other departments, or other team members when problems arise, leads to mediocrity and poor performance. A philosophy of continuous improvement, a "creative dissatisfaction" mindset, helps you embrace the opportunity for improvement and innovation that problems offer.

We have accepted the idea that problems reflect inadequacies in people—the problems must be our fault or someone else's. This attitude creates an atmosphere that leads to naming, blaming, and shaming when a problem arises—"It must be Bill's fault."

Instead of the natural response of finding the "bad person," you must ask what went wrong—what is missing or broken in our processes?

Problems are normal; all enterprises encounter problems. The difference between good companies and excellent companies is how they approach, solve, and learn from problems.

Meltdown

Kirk, the maintenance manager for a Portland-area manufacturer, told us,

> We experienced a major meltdown in the plant this last week. Machine #5's headbox froze and brought production to a standstill. It wasn't the first time, and it was just as bad as ever, but there was something different this time. The difference was the way I handled it. This time, I responded instead of reacted.
>
> Instead of losing my temper, trying to point out who was wrong, I focused on trying to discover the root cause of the problem, finding out how and where our system failed.

Remember, reacting is when we act without thinking—it's a knee-jerk action. Shouting and blaming sets up a scenario: you react, and then the person you've attacked reacts in defense. These combative reactions eliminate any possibility for significant, permanent, continuous performance improvements. Even if you finally solve the problem, relationships are so damaged that performance suffers, sometimes for years.

It's in responding, not reacting, that you help people become more open, willing to admit problems exist. You help those on the front lines become capable problem solvers. When you include people closest to the problem in your search for the root cause and the best solution, you make them more aware of how they can keep future problems from occurring. This helps everyone on the team be open and responsive to changes in processes, methods, and procedures.

Continuous Improvement Culture

The engaging leader's role is to create a culture where everyone is committed to continuous improvement. Defensiveness is replaced with responsiveness to even the slightest symptom of a problem. How do you do this? You must communicate your belief in the philosophy of continuous improvement as a path to superior customer service and competitive advantage.

Create an environment where everyone is encouraged to say "I think we may have a problem," instead of waiting for things to blow completely out of proportion. Instead of waiting for someone else to report the problem, people on the front line feel empowered to say "Whoops, something's not working."

Simple, yet this is not the traditional approach taken by most organizations. Too often we have "killed the messenger." Top managers can "kill the messenger" and send the signal to "keep your head down" with dogmatic comments like, "You know better than that," "I can't believe you let that happen," "Couldn't you see that coming?" "What's wrong with you, anyway?" "That's not a problem." "We've always done it that way." "You don't understand."

You create engagement when you make heroes out of the people who report problems. Show your appreciation in a public way, thanking them at team meetings or mentioning them in team newsletters. Empower the people closest to the problem, who first observe the symptom of a problem, whether it's a part out of place or a piece of information that doesn't seem quite right, to stop the process before more costs are piled on. This principle applies to any kind of process: Everything we do involves processes: manufacturing, buying, billing, planning and coordinating events or projects, shipping and receiving, advertising, and public relations.

Why wait until a project has passed through a half-dozen more value-added stages before saying, "This is wrong, this won't work"? Worse yet, why wait for your customer to be your quality control department by complaining about an incorrect invoice or returning a defective item and asking for a credit, or worse, doing business with your competitor instead of you?

By empowering your team to stop the process, "shut down the line," you may be amazed at how many errors you begin to eliminate, how much money you save, and how much additional positive engagement you create. Your team will increasingly be engaged and committed to "doing it right the first time."

> *"We'll never solve the problems we don't talk about."*
> Justin Young

Probing the Probes Problem

Ron, thermomechanical pulping (TMP) supervisor for a paper mill in northern Ontario, Canada, told us,

A few weeks ago our R2 reject refiner plates crashed. They had been in operation less than 24 hours! This was a huge letdown for the entire mill. Our TMP personnel were especially frustrated. The mill had been struggling to manufacture quality pulp with the old plates, which we had removed from the refiner just the day before. The new plates were expected to make life much easier, and, instead, things had just gotten worse, much worse, with little hope in sight.

After over 12 hours, we were finally able to isolate the root cause of the problem. We traced the cause back to a defective rebuilt TDC probe. A TDC probe is an electronic device that measures plate gap. Because the plates cost in excess of $30,000 each, Operations was now tasked with finding ways to make quality pulp with the damaged plates. This is a very frustrating and cumbersome process. Operating with damaged plates is non-textbook and requires the constant attention of an experienced, skilled operator, making good judgments moment by moment.

Many of our operations and maintenance personnel were frustrated because this was a repeat failure. Rather than letting myself get frustrated, joining in the angst, I used my adrenaline and energy to gather the facts. I was able to put together sufficient data to prove that the cost of a rebuilt probe was actually more than the cost of a new one. Armed with these facts, I could help mill management justify replacing the rebuilt probes with lower cost and more reliable new probes. The automatic tracking system has since been changed to eliminate repeat failures, reduce demand for maintenance resources, and lower our overall operating costs.

The lesson I learned from this experience is that getting mad is a waste of energy. When I apply my energy to productive fact-finding research, I can be part of the solution. Getting angry doesn't solve problems. It only makes me a part of the problem.

Remaining centered helps ensure clear thinking, making it possible to learn from problems, and your gains are sustained. A part of maturity is learning that we live in a world we cannot completely control. The only thing we have complete control of is our attitude, our response to life's breakdowns. By learning to control your attitude, you are an empowered leader that solves problems and contributes to the creation of an engaged, victorious team.

The Problem Statement

My experience shows that when people are asked to state a problem, 75 percent will instead state the cause or the solution to a problem. They prescribe medicine before they have accurately defined the problem and long before they've found the true root cause.

Let's look at some familiar problems. Say you come home from a movie and walk into your kitchen. There is an inch of water on the floor, the sink is overflowing, and no one else is there. A stack of dishes is in the sink, apparently blocking the drain. Which of the following is the definition of the problem?

1. Turn off the water.
2. The drain is blocked.
3. Somebody left the kitchen with the water running.
4. Unexpectedly, there is an inch of water on the floor.

The first—turn off the water—is an appropriate action, but it is not a definition of the problem. Turning the faucet off addresses the symptom of the problem, and you still have water on the floor and a sink that can't be used.

The second—the drain is blocked—is a cause statement. It does not describe the problem, but leaps right to a cause, which may or may not be the root cause.

The third—someone left the kitchen with the water running—suggests preventive action to head off a future problem like this, but it won't help us with this problem.

The fourth—unexpectedly, there is an inch of water on the floor—is a definition of the problem. It describes the current state that was not expected.

Just like an accurate diagnosis by a capable doctor, a problem statement identifies what is wrong. As the first step, it focuses on what *is*, not on why or how it got that way—the cause—or how to fix it—the solution.

> *"The framing of a problem is often*
> *far more essential than its solution."*
> Albert Einstein

Rooting out the Root Cause

Here's another scenario: a credit must be written because a wrong part was shipped. What's the problem? Simple: your client received the wrong part. In doing an investigation, you discover that the parts are in the wrong bin. Is the root cause of the shipment error that the item was in the wrong bin? Are you sure? *Why* was the item in the wrong bin? Poor labeling? New packaging? New stock clerk? Poor training? Poor lighting?

The root cause is the cause that's really at the root of the problem, the most basic underlying cause that can be identified and fixed to prevent a recurrence of the problem.

You've probably heard the rhyme about the kingdom lost "for want of a nail." It's often used to illustrate the enormous effects that small details can have—in this case, the lack of one nail for a horseshoe leads to the loss of a kingdom. Here's one version of it:

> *For want of a nail the shoe was lost,*
> *for want of a shoe the horse was lost,*
> *for want of a horse the knight was lost,*
> *for want of a knight the battle was lost,*
> *for want of a battle the kingdom was lost,*
> *and all for want of a horseshoe nail.*

This rhyme can also remind us that the root cause of a problem might not be obvious. We may need to investigate several layers before we find the "missing nail."

On-Track Problem Solving

Following is a simple five-step model to put your problem-solving process on track:

1. Define the problem. "A problem well-stated is a problem half-solved!"[24] Remember: a problem statement accurately describes the current unexpected state. It's not a question—it's a statement. Your well-stated problem will pinpoint the issue with specificity and won't include the cause or the solution. "Our client received the wrong part."

2. Identify the root cause. Don't jump to solutions—just causes now. Look at every option; drop your defensiveness. Be open to all *possible* causes of the problem. Give up your ego, your special interests, and your biases about people, methods, and procedures. Brainstorm or research the possible causes. This will allow your team to identify the many possible causes without judging why they exist. The brainstorming approach can help eliminate defensive cover-up tactics. It also helps the team ultimately identify the real root cause among all the possible causes examined.

3. List all possible solutions to the problem. Don't jump to conclusions—just possible solutions now. As your team brainstorms, listen, really listen, to every possible solution. Realize that there are at least ten solutions to every problem. Here we want quantity, not quality. No judgment of the solution being presented.

4. Identify the best possible solution. After your team has generated all possible solutions, look at options in light of resources (time, talent, capital, etc.) to determine the best possible solution—the one that will work best now. This can be accomplished through consensus or a majority-vote.

5. Execute—put the solution into action. You must take action or all of the thought, work, and planning goes down the drain—another wasted meeting. This is perhaps the greatest demotivator of what would otherwise be high-performance teams. Determine what actions must be taken to implement the solution. Identify who is responsible to implement the action plan, how it will be implemented, and when it will be implemented.

A last word of advice: make sure the people affected by the problem and those required to implement the solution are willing to cooperate. Solutions don't work in a vacuum. People implement solutions, and their feelings, fears, interests, and biases must be considered when deciding on solutions.

This process, when properly followed, leads to unified action by your engaged team. Involve your team in the above process and your solutions will be accepted and acted upon.

Facilitating Group Problem Solving

Your job as the facilitator of a problem-solving conference is not to solve the problem or come up with all the ideas. Your job is to be sure you stimulate the maximum number of ideas from everyone in your group and ensure everyone is heard. To gain full involvement, here are a few suggestions:

- Make certain that everyone in your group participates. If you have someone who seems to be holding back, ask, "Jill, what do you think?"
- Never permit criticism, evaluation, or judgment when you are collecting ideas.
- Use neutral tones when you ask, "How would that work?" "How do you mean that?" "Can you give us an example?"
- Original thought must be stimulated or you will remain stuck in the conventionality of the past. Include outsiders—people from outside your department, area, or company. Ask someone who is blissfully ignorant of standard practice, who don't know why "it can't be done," to participate in your meeting. Invite people to participate who don't have a personal stake in the outcome.
- By encouraging wild ideas, you develop useable innovations.

  "The improvisational ability to lead adaptively relies on responding to the present situation rather than importing the past into the present and laying it on the current situation like an imperfect template."
  Ronald A. Heifetz

Problem-solving is endless. You must never stop exploring for better ways. This is one of the most important habits your team can develop. It ensures continuous improvement.

Excuses Don't Look Good on Me

As team members carry out the action plans decided upon, it's extremely important to make clear to them that "we will keep our commitments." Renegotiate deadlines when they can't be met. As I point out in *Repeat Business*, "Excuses don't look good on me." Any time we find ourselves not able to keep our commitments, the next thing we find ourselves doing is making up excuses. To avoid excuse-making, when committed-to deadlines can't be met, renegotiate completion times and recommit to the new date. If anyone senses that others are blowing off commitments, they'll know they can't rely on other team members or other departments. You'll instantly lose their engagement.

Decision Making

Not all decisions are tied to problems. Starting new ventures, exploiting unforeseen opportunities, and achieving continuous improvement requires *new decisions*. At its simplest level, decision-making means choosing one option out of several choices.

You must acquire the habit of making decisions. You must dispose rapidly of the dozens of little problems that come up every day. The way you do this is to make decisions. Right or wrong, make a decision!

You don't always have to make the right decision. What matters is to make the decision. Force yourself on to the next one rather than getting stuck worrying about whether your decision is "right." This is the only way you can acquire the desired quality of decisiveness. Once you acquire this habit of decisiveness, you step into the top ten percent—the "doers," the top leaders.

When you are on the firing line of decision making, you are a winner! Sound judgment is acquired only by the habit of decisive decision making. You learn from experience and the outcome of your decisions. You must start making decisions now. You must *act*, and act *quickly*!

> *"We need to accept that we won't always make the right decisions, that we'll screw up royally sometimes—understanding that failure is not the opposite of success, it's part of success."*
> Arianna Huffington

Opportunity Buffet

I can't leave the subject of problem solving without asking you to adopt the philosophy apparent in the following idea from John E. Jones and William Bearley:

Eat problems for lunch. Leaders need to consider the situations that arise in work areas as opportunities for improvement rather than as headaches or distractions. Problems can be their best teachers. . . . Leaders need to communicate this positive attitude."[25]

> *"Problems are only opportunities in work clothes."*
> Henry J. Kaiser

Actions for Engaging Leaders

- When problems occur, don't drain your energy getting frustrated.
- Use your energy in a productive way to find solutions.
- Make decisions.

Benefits You Will Gain

- You will see improvement in processes and results.
- You'll develop the desirable habit of decisiveness.
- You will improve your ability to make good decisions.

"Nothing stops people who desire to achieve. Every obstacle is simply a course to develop their achievement muscles. It's a strengthening of their powers of accomplishment."
Eric Butterworth

Leaders Are Learners

I'll never forget early in my career sitting in the convention center in downtown Detroit, listening with rapt attention to Earl Nightingale's classic presentation, "The Strangest Secret." At one point he said, "I can tell you how you can become smarter than your boss and perform at a higher level than anyone you work with today." He had my full attention— I was listening!

He continued. "Simply devote 20 minutes every morning to studying your craft. If you were investing in a company for the long term—20 or 30 years, through retirement—I'd recommend you invest in a company that has an active research and development department, one that puts back at least ten percent of its earnings into new product development. For you to be successful, you must have your own research and development department. Put ten percent of your income and time into your own personal growth, and you'll be a long-term success."

I have followed his advice.

I urge you as a leader to set aside time to be a learner. Don't wait for your company to send you to programs. Search outside of your industry for ideas to improve your abilities.

Personal development will stimulate your creativity and bring you new insights for increased opportunities and expanded responsibilities.

All significant breakthroughs offer leaders as learners new paths to follow. The trick is to be in front of the curve, recognize these new opportunities before they happen. Too often, the closer we are to opportunities, the blinder we become. One example is Yahoo!'s hesitation in 2006 during negotiations to buy Facebook. After a handshake agreement between Yahoo! CEO Terry Semel and Facebook's Mark Zuckerberg for a $1 billion buyout, Yahoo! made a counter-offer of $800 million instead. Even when Yahoo! re-offered the $1 billion price a few weeks later, Zuckerberg, having had second thoughts, declined.[26]

Here's another example: Xerox engineers created the first computer to use a graphical user interface and a mouse in 1973, but was slow to capitalize on its creation. Xerox's second iteration of the computer was launched in 1981, but by then the company was already far behind Apple in the development and marketing of personal computers.[27]

Being aware of breakthroughs in technology, medicine, science, nanotechnology, and energy helps ready you for the market disruptions that come faster and faster. You must ready yourself or you will be left behind. Most important, learn to learn from your own experiences. Force yourself to do what I have urged the thousands of Leadership Development Lab participants to do for decades—at the culmination of every significant event, ask yourself this question, "What have I learned from this experience?" Ask again until you discover the operating principle that will guide you to continued success.

At the close of every day, ask, "What was the most important event in my life today, and what can I learn from it?"

Vision Enhancement

When I walked into the Water Tower Eye Clinic for my annual eye examination, I was wearing bifocals. I had stopped wearing my contacts a few months earlier because it was too much hassle to wear them—they only corrected my distance vision so I still had to search for my reading glasses all the time. As far as I could see, there was only one answer—to start wearing my old bifocals again. I asked my optometrist about bifocal contacts and he confirmed what I had heard: "They just don't seem to work very well." After my examination, he said, "Let's see how this works." He popped in a couple of contacts. I could see to read, and I could see at a distance. What had he done? A new combination—a contact in one eye for reading, and one in the other eye for distance. I'm wearing them today— I can read and see to drive.

The lesson I learned from this experience is I must open myself to all possibilities. I must be willing to open my eyes, to see things differently. As engaging leaders, we have the responsibility to open our eyes to new possibilities, new answers to old problems, new combinations. Examine possibilities up close and take a hard look at them from a distance, push them away for a new perspective. As you open yourself to new options and fresh combinations, you'll find better ways to accomplish your goals. You'll experience continuous improvements, and that's what makes you an engaging leader.

Keep Pedaling

I recently had dinner in Yakima, WA, with Greg Luring. He and his wife, Jan, own 11 McDonald's stores in the Yakima Valley. With heartfelt enthusiasm and an earned air of achievement, Greg told me about riding his bicycle back to Ohio for his 30th class reunion:

This is a 2,350-mile trip. It took exactly five weeks and I rode every day but two. I didn't reach 100 miles per day until after two weeks. My best day was 135 miles. One mental state of mind really helped me—I decided that I would rent a car if it looked like I wouldn't make it back to Bellefontaine, OH, in time. I would drive to the reunion, then drive back to where I rented the car and finish the ride. Knowing that I was going to finish one way or another kept me focused and, indeed, I did finish the ride one day before the reunion. My 75-year-old father arranged for a police escort into town.

Greg knew how many miles per day he had to average in order to arrive on schedule. He rode by himself and rented hotel rooms each night. He said when he fell behind and it looked like he wasn't going to make it on time, his agreement with himself kept him going. It was this level of commitment that gave him the drive he needed to get up at the crack of dawn and keep on pedaling. With this extra measure of committed determination, he made it. Greg lost 35 pounds on the grueling five-week trip. Jan, who had flown to Ohio, and several of his high school buddies and friends came out to meet him as he crossed into Bellefontaine city limits. They gave Greg a hero's welcome.

Greg told me, "Words can't describe how exhilarating it was to 'cross the finish line.'" Greg's sense of achievement can't be won or inherited; you can't marry into it or win it in the lottery. This sense of achievement can only be earned. Greg said, "The lesson I learned is that when I make a non-compromising commitment to a stretch goal that has rewards and consequences built in, I achieve far more than seems physically possible."

Tomorrow is Unknown

I was the presenter at a teacher education day. When the district superintendent introduced me, he said, "We must stop trying to turn out students to fill specific jobs. The young people who are in our schools will not have just one job. We may have chosen teaching careers early in our lives and may teach all of our lives. In this era of rapid change, our students are likely to have three, four, or more careers. They will have jobs that don't even exist today. So our most important responsibility is to help them learn how to learn."

You must learn how to squeeze every ounce of insight possible from every experience. The old model of learning how to do a job and then doing it for the rest of your life is as out of date as the manual typewriters, 10-key adding machines, and mimeograph machines sold in the early '40s and '50s.

Life-long Learners

Leaders are readers. This means that you are reading the books, magazines, newsletters, and blogs that relate directly to your field and those outside your professional discipline to find the ideas and concepts you can adapt to your business. Supplement print material with audio-reports and audiobooks.

As I backed out of the garage this morning, I continued listening to the book I was listening to when I pulled into the garage the night before. This is nothing new for me: it's my daily routine. As a subscriber to Audio Tech Business Book Summaries (www.audiotech.com) and Business Briefings (www.briefings.audiotech.com) and an avid listener to The Great Courses (www.thegreatcourses.com) and Celebration Church's Sunday CDs, I turn my driving time into learning time. I consider my car a classroom on wheels.

According to the American Automobile Association, the average driver clocks 12,000 to 25,000 miles each year. This means you're spending 500 to 1,000 hours in your car each year. That is the equivalent of 12½ to 25 forty-hour weeks or two *full* university semesters spent behind the wheel of your car each year.

Time management is the central personal skill of success. Your ability to manage your time, to focus and channel your energies on your highest-value tasks, determines your rewards and level of accomplishment more than any other factor. If you made no other change but started using your traveling time as learning time, this decision alone could make you, as Earl Nightingale said, "smarter than your boss." Many people have significantly improved their prospects simply by listening to audio programs as they drove to and from work.

In addition, for personal and professional development, you should attend every seminar you can, a minimum of one a year. You can often save yourself hundreds of hours of reading and researching by attending a seminar given by an authority in your field. You can learn ideas, techniques, and methods that can save you hours, days, even months of hard work and research on your own.

Remember: to earn more, you must learn more. Your outer world of results will always correspond to your inner world of preparation. Continuous learning is the minimum requirement for success in any field.

Authentic Learning

For over 18 months, I recorded a daily 45-second motivational message for those who called in to get a lift. It was a big job to find a kernel in some incident from the previous day that inspired a message to pass on to others. This kind of learning is what I call "Authentic Learning." Discussing your learning experience with others at the close of your day can be one of the most empowering things you can do. When you've reached an understanding with yourself about what you've learned from the incidents in your life, sharing your understanding with others will help clarify and deepen your own learning.

Sometimes when we reach narrow conclusions based on our experiences, we repeat the same mistakes over and over.

Of course, it's easier to notice repeated mistakes in others than in ourselves. Forcing yourself to analyze each important event that happens in your life will ultimately help you learn more from your experiences.

Beyond the Zone

Continuing to push yourself beyond your comfort zone is one of the most important things you can do to stimulate your learning. Taking risks, going beyond where you're comfortable to the place of uncertainty, is where you really learn. Those places that surpass your old self, the person who thinks "this is just the way I am," will help you redefine yourself as someone who is dynamic, changing, learning, and growing.

> *"I learned to always take on things I'd never done before. Growth and comfort do not coexist."*
> Virginia Rommetty[28]

Dual Systems

Lisa, corporate finance director for a commercial heating and air conditioning service contractor, told us how being a learner helped her with an important transition in office technology:

> We are an HVAC service provider and are part of an international network of LINC Service Franchises. LINC provides its contractors with the tools and software systems needed to run a successful service business.
>
> Back in mid-1997, my boss and I decided it was time to take our company out of the "dark ages" (the dark ages being an IBM Main Frame system) and into a more modern era of technology by converting over to the latest version of software that LINC provided.
>
> LINC urged its affiliate contractors who were converting their software to go "cold turkey"—basically

shut off the old and start up the new. Following this recommendation, our sister construction company went several thousand dollars over budget on their software conversion. We knew we did not want to follow in their footsteps. We decided that we should run dual systems for one month. Then, if all went well, we would go ahead and pull the plug on the old system.

Once that decision was made, I spent the next several months pushing LINC hard for information: What went well during prior conversions they had run? What didn't go well? What data was going to convert automatically? What data wasn't going to convert and would therefore require further action after the installation was completed? Based on what I learned, I formulated timelines and action plans for everyone that would be involved in the conversion of our data.

We had made the decision that we did not want to manage our business from two different sets of financials for the 12 months following the conversion. Because December is our fiscal year end, that was the month we ran our conversion. Once we had run the conversion, I brought in temporary workers to assist us with hand keying in all the job cost history data for all of our client contracts. Then I, along with my staff of one, commenced entering all of the accounts payable, accounts receivable, and general ledger journal entries into both systems.

It took me two months to close December, but when I did, I had matching year-end financials in both systems. But, best of all, I knew how our new system operated from the inside out.

In March of 1998 during our annual Continuing Education Conference, in front of several hundred of my network peers, LINC thanked me for helping them improve upon their conversion process. They recognized me as their 1997 Business Systems Manager of the year, across the entire national contractor network!

"The lesson I learned from this experience is that there truly are no shortcuts to excellence."

Lobster

I found fascinating insights about learning and risk in an article by Eda LeShan. LeShan describes meeting an oceanographer while she was writing *The Wonderful Crisis of Middle Age*. He told her that the only way a lobster can grow is to regularly shed its shell. The pink membrane covering the lobster hardens and becomes the next shell, but in the meantime, the lobster is very vulnerable. "In other words," says LeShan, "a lobster has to risk its life in order to grow." LeShan then makes the point that people aren't so different:

> We all know when our shells have gotten too tight. We feel angry or depressed or frightened because life is no longer exciting or challenging. . . . or we are doing things we hate to do and are feeling stifled in our shells. Some of us continue to smother in old shells that are no longer useful or productive. That way we can at least feel safe—nothing can happen to us. Others are luckier; even though we know we will be vulnerable—that there are dangers ahead—we realize that we must take risks or suffocate.[29]

As an empowering leader, you are growing. Ask yourself if it is time to stretch "lobster-like" and reach for the next step in your personal growth. Stretching will keep you young and your mind flexible. Wake up your napping synapses!

Learning and Growing

Within every experience there is a lesson for us and others to learn. Although the possibility to learn from every experience exists, we actually learn from only a few. How can we change this? How do we turn our lives into a classroom, a laboratory to learn from and make every day another meaningful rung on the ladder to success?

1. Acknowledge that you can learn and grow regardless of your age, your level of formal education, or your schedule.
2. Believe you *can* learn from all your experiences—those you call good and those experiences you aren't even aware of, those you sometimes sleepwalk through.
3. Take full responsibility for everything that happens in your life—not blaming others, circumstances, or powers outside of your control.
4. Look for the lesson you can learn in all your experiences.
5. Look for the principle operating beneath the experience. Believe you live in an orderly, consistent universe, a world of cause and effect, where nothing happens by accident, where there are no random events.
6. Express the experience and the lesson learned. Until you can verbalize or write about your experience and lesson learned, you haven't fully understood your experience. You haven't truly "experienced the experience." Expressing your lesson will clarify and crystallize your learning.

Happy Birthday

I have good memories of when our extended family gathered at the Country Meadows Retirement Village in Woodburn to celebrate my mother's 93rd birthday. She was an amazing woman.

While waiting for her to join us in the community room, we met 85-year-old Charles, a relatively new resident. He was energetic, outgoing, and eager to talk. He had a great voice. My brother Bruce asked him if he had ever been in radio. With a big smile, he said, "No." We asked him what he did before he retired. He responded, "Well, that's a long story" and launched into a fairly comprehensive overview of his biography. When he was 15 years old, he ran off to join the Air Force and ultimately was a fighter pilot in World War II.

Charles missed out on our family singing "Happy Birthday." When he came around later, he gave my mother a solo version of "Happy Birthday," followed by his own rendition of "Let Me Call You Sweetheart." My brother queried him again about his secret of a happy, successful life. He mentioned something about a card that had a message on it from his mother, Rosa.

Then he said, "I'll let you guys get back to your party" and went on his way. A few minutes later, he returned with a beautiful calligraphy version of his mother's philosophy, a powerful affirmation.

> "Keep a small dream in the making. It need'nt be big or bold, just some little dream to beckon you on, and you will never, no never, grow old".
>
> Grandma Rosa Karl
> (*Rosa lived to be 101½ years old.*)

How can you argue with success? Rosa lived to be 101½! We know intuitively the rightness of this philosophy. We know the importance of having something to live for, something to look forward to. We talk to people every day, it seems, who, when asked about what's going on or how they are, say "Same old, same old," "Just getting by," and other neutral to negative comments about their life, work, and state of their world. So if you'd like to live to be 101½ and, more importantly, *live* every day of your life, why not adopt Rosa Karl's affirmation: "*Keep a small dream in the making.*"

Actions for Engaging Leaders

- Resolve to turn driving time into learning time.
- Seek out seminars and training programs given by experts in your field.
- Write down your dream, a stretch goal you can commit to. Read it every day. Develop a plan to take a step toward realizing your dream.

Benefits You Will Gain

- Your enjoyment of life and work will steadily grow.
- You will gain a sense of accomplishment that will stay with you for the rest of your life.
- You'll be amazed at what happens.

"Do not be too timid and squeamish about your actions. All life is an experiment. The more experiments you make the better. What if they are a little coarse, and you may get your coat soiled or torn? What if you do fail, and get fairly rolled in the dirt once or twice? Up again, you shall never be so afraid of a tumble."

Ralph Waldo Emerson

>>>Notes

[1] From "What is Engagement" by Kevin Kruse. Forbes.com. 6/22/2012.

[2] From "What is Employee Engagement." EngageforSuccess.org.

[3] In "Employee Engagement Does More than Boost Productivity" by John Baldoni. Harvard Business Review Blog Network. 7/4/2013.

[4] "The X Model of Employee Engagement: Satisfaction and Contribution." BlessingWhite.com. 2014.

[5] "How Employee Engagement Drives Growth" by Susan Sorenson. Gallup Business Journal. http://www.gallup.com/businessjournal/163130/employee-engagement-drives-growth.aspx. 6/20/2013.

[6] Joel Barker, *Future Edge* (New York: William Morrow, 1992).

[7] Theodore Levitt, "Marketing Myopia," *Harvard Business Review* 38 (July/Aug. 1960).

[8] Dec. 23, 1844 Correspondence from Micheltorena to Sutter, quoted in *History of California: 1884-90* by Hubert Howe Bancroft (Charlston: Nabu Press, 2010, reprint) p. 474, footnote 29.

[9] Full title is *Predicting Executive Success: What It Takes to Make It into Senior Mangement* (Wiley, 1985).

[10] Quoted by Ted Owen in "Words of wisdom still inspire 100 years later." *Carlsbad Business Journal*, 1 May 2014, www.carlsbad.org.

[11] "Appreciate," Wikipedia.com.

[12] From Andor Földes, "Beethoven's Kiss," *Reader's Digest*, Nov. 1986. 145.

[13] E.T. Webb and J.J.B. Morgan, *Strategy in Handling People* (New York: Garden City Publishing Co. 1930), 83. "Man" replaced with "person" and "leader."

[14] E.T. Webb and J.J.B. Morgan, *Strategy in Handling People* (New York: Garden City Publishing Co. 1930), 123. "Man" and "men" replaced with "person" and "people" or "leader(s)."

[15] J.P. Guildford, "Creativity," *American Psychologist.* Sept. 1950. 448.

[16] Alex F. Osborn, *Applied Imagination* (New York: Scribner, 1979), 286-287.

[17] "Celebrate," Merriam-Webster Online.

[18] For a complete explanation of Turbo's 3-Step On-the-Job Training Process, read *The Language of Leadership: Communicating for Results* by Larry Dennis (Rising Tide Publishing, 2010).

[19] "Lose," www.thefreedictionary.com.

[20] This YouTube video is a graphic example of the high cost of not managing complaints properly: http://youtu.be/5YGc4zOqozo

[21] Turbo Leadership System's 5-Step DARE+ Correction Process is explained in chapter 11 of *The Language of Leadership: Communicating for Results* by Larry Dennis (Rising Tide Publishing, 2010), pp. 203-225. Here it is briefly:

> **D**escribe the observed unacceptable behavior
>
> **A**sk "What happened?" Listen carefully to the response.
>
> **R**estate the agreed-to standard
>
> **E**mphasize the reason the standard is important + Ask for their agreement to perform to the standard
>
> + End on a positive note

[22] For a complete explanation of Turbo's 3-Step On-the-Job Training Process, read *The Language of Leadership: Communicating for Results* by Larry Dennis (Rising Tide Publishing, 2010).

[23] H. Jackson Brown is the author of *Life's Little Instruction Book* (Thomas Nelson, 2012).

[24] Quote attributed to both John Dewey ("problem well put" or "problem well defined") and Charles Kettering ("problem well stated").

[25] John E. Jones & William Bearley, *360 Feedback: Strategies, Tactics, and Techniques for Developing Leaders* (Amherst: HRD Press, 1996), 6.

[26] From "5 Businesses That Missed Out Big-Time" by Joe Mont. www.TheStreet.com. 6 Dec. 2011. Accessed 12 Nov. 2014.

[27] Also from "5 Businesses That Missed Out Big-Time" (see above).

[28] CEO of IBM.

[29] In *Women's Day Magazine*. 22 Sept. 1981.

About the Author

Larry W. Dennis, Sr. is the energetic founder of Turbo Leadership Systems™, headquartered in the metro Portland, Oregon, area and has been helping businesses in the US and Canada improve their performance for over 29 years.

Larry began Turbo Leadership Systems with proven sales and leadership experience. For fifteen years, he was a top performer with the Ralph Nichols Corporation, ranking number one in the world in their Sales Course production. He also earned awards in sales in Illinois and Oregon.

Larry is a life-long learner and has used his expertise to design customized interventions, leading to the improved performance and profits of hundreds of organizations. He helps leaders develop confident skills in communication, teamwork, customer service, and engaging leadership.

A dedicated father, and grandfather of seven, Larry has been profiled in "Secrets of Raising Teenagers Successfully." He is listed in *Who's Who of the World*, serves on his church board, the Providence Newberg Health Foundation, and the Cascade Policy Institute board, and is a member of the International Platform Association. He is the author of ten inspiring books.

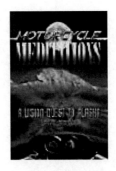

Motorcycle Meditations: A Vision Quest to Alaska
Share Larry W. Dennis, Sr.'s adventure of a lifetime. Ride along and experience his journey through Canada on the Al-Can and on through Alaska to Anchorage and Homer. You will experience the power of positive introspection, reflect on your own life, and rediscover the gifts your life has given you. You will see with fresh eyes the promise of your future.
ISBN 0-9631766-6-8 $19.95

15 Leadership Principles and Ronald Reagan: Use Them to Change Your World is designed to inspire the leader reader to confidently set the agenda for breakthrough step change for their company, department, or precinct as Ronald Reagan did for the United States and the world. Championing change is never easy. It requires vision, communication skills, and the courage to act as the fearful stand on the sidelines.
Second Printing   ISBN 0-9631766-9-1 $19.95

Making Moments Matter: 89 Tools for Taking Charge of Your Time provides powerful time management tools to help you become more organized and productive in your professional and personal lives. 89 time management tools provide insight into how to make the most of every precious minute of every day.

Third Printing   ISBN 0-9631766-4-4 $16.95

InFormation: How to Gain the 71% Advantage equips your team with the same advantage a flock of geese takes for granted. By following the tested guidelines outlined in this authentic resource book, your organization will fly farther, faster, and with no additional effort, keeping your team out in front.

Third Printing   ISBN 0-9631766-3-3 $19.95

How to Turbocharge You: 6 Steps to Tap Your True Potential guides you to an understanding of your unique talents and abilities. You see for the first time how to leverage your past successes. Written with real life examples, in an entertaining style, *How to Turbocharge You* equips you with the 14 tools needed to thrive in a time of uncertainty and accelerated change.

Fourth Printing   ISBN 0-9631766-2-5 $14.95

Repeat Business: 6 Steps to Superior Customer Service teaches your new and long-term employees the skills that will help you create loyal customers. Written in straightforward language with colorful anecdotes, *Repeat Business* helps you learn how to treat customers so they keep coming back as satisfied clients.

Sixth Printing   ISBN 0-9631766-0-9 $9.95

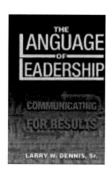

The Language of Leadership: Communicating for Results helps you dramatically improve your communication effectiveness, increasing your value as an engaging leader. Communication is the foundational skill required to successfully maximize the value of all resources. Twelve chapters provide specific insights on how to improve communication in every area of your life

First Printing   ISBN 0-9631766-8-4 $19.95

The Great Baseball Cap

This 32-page character-building children's story is illustrated with warm 5-color pencil drawings. *The Great Baseball Cap* inspires 4 to 10-year-old readers to take pride in their personal appearance, value relationships with their parents, siblings, and friends, and most important of all, value themselves. *The Great Baseball Cap* literally takes the young reader to the point of affirming "I AM A WINNER!"

ISBN 0-9631766-5-X $9.95

TURBO LEADERSHIP SYSTEMS PROCESSES

Cultural Benchmark Survey™ (CBS): Developed with the Industrial Psychology Department at Roosevelt University, the CBS is an easy-to-use, state-of-the-art analytical process. We scale the strengths and weaknesses of your organization and identify the priority actions to help you immediately improve quality, customer satisfaction, processes and profits for the long term. This low-cost, proven innovative system ensures future initiatives are calculated to concentrate on the areas that require the greatest attention.

Leadership Team Advance™ (LTA): Your senior leadership team aligns to "concentrate on the vital few and ignore the trivial many." The two-day offsite is preceded by peer surveys and includes a built-in 90-day follow-up accountability session to ensure immediate, profitable action is taken.

Cultural Quality Awareness™ (CQA): Overcomes cultural resistance to change and creates energized action. A strong decided signal is sent. Everyone understands the magnitude of the challenges faced and commits to their part in making productive, profitable changes.

Quality Steering Team™ (QST): Ensures the focused buy-in required for your improvement effort to have long-term successful impact and continuously closes the communication loop between all constituencies. The QST champions your improvement effort and ensures new issues are addressed in a timely manner.

Leadership Development Lab™ (LDL): Creating "culture change"—implementing a continuous improvement process to reduce costs, improve quality, and enhance customer satisfaction—is only successful when all key team members are committed to their own personal growth. The 10-week LDL ensures your leadership team takes the initiative in *Communicating the Vision* and *Providing Empowering Encouragement, Constructive Coaching, Courageous Correction,* and more. Your leaders develop the ability to both give and get the authority necessary to improve performance at every level. This shared ownership results in the improved cross-departmental teamwork required for continuous improvement.

Performance Team Lab™ (PTL): You engage everyone in your organization over a 12-month period in the pursuit of continuous improvement. All departments accept as a part of their job the improvement of processes and the final outcome of their work. You redefine the role of the department manager to team leader and coach. You stimulate improvement through scorekeeping, process analysis, and problem solving to achieve the highest possible quality at the lowest effective cost.

Continuous Improvement Coaching™ (CIC): Sustains your commitment to continued improvement in targeted areas where ongoing development is needed, including customer service, sales, supervision, process improvement, problem solving, staffing, strategic planning, and time management. Quarterly follow-up sessions are individually tailored to your current needs as revealed by the follow-up Cultural Benchmark Survey (CBS).

Construction Partnering for Success (CPS): Partnering reframes and moves owners, contractors, engineers, and inspectors from confrontation to alliance—a pledge of cooperation and teamwork.

Ac SELL erators

Customer Service LAB™ (CSL): Your customer associates develop the skills to make their work more rewarding—greeting the customer, asking questions, selling benefits, handling complaints, and expressing gratitude. Your customers see you as reliable, responsive and resourceful, going the extra mile to exceed their expectations. You see your repeat business and average sales ticket grow as your customer satisfaction scores improve.

Turbo Sales System (TSS): Through improved skills and a clearer understanding of the buyer's decision-making process, your salespeople attain greater success. Drill-for-skills on first impressions, determining need, selling benefits, using evidence, answering objections, and getting action results in increased sales. These skills are honed over 10 weeks through participation and application in day-to-day selling.

Turbocharging Your Sales Force (TSF) Your sales managers develop a sophisticated process approach to creating a high performance sales team—track and keep score of lead indicators, analyze their market, identify the "A" prospects, and coach sales reps to peak performance, which results in growing sales and profits.

"Empowering your team to ensure continuous improvement."

For more information about Turbo Leadership Systems' programs, please contact us.

Turbo Leadership Systems
10195 SW Alsea Ct
Tualatin, OR 97062

Phone: (503) 691-2867
Fax: (503) 691-5434

www.turbols.com
admin@turbols.com

To order books, please visit www.turbols.com/turbo_books.html